Here's What Readers and Reviewers Say About

The Art of Managing...
How to Build a Better Workplace
and Relationships

"Macken's slim little volume is a wonderful melding of management theory and psychology. I expect it to benefit both new managers who are seeking to understand a discipline that is often quite different than their education prepared them for and experienced managers looking for new ways to analyze and improve their effectiveness. For that reason, I expect to keep a large supply in stock to replace my own copy as I give it away."

Jeanne Sheldon, Corporate Vice President,
Microsoft Corporation

"This is an excellent book for managers and students of management who want exposure to the spectrum of theory and practice that can make a difference in management effectiveness. Jane Macken introduces the reader to an amazing number of concepts in a way that is interesting and practical. Her focus on what managers need to know and understand about self and others is key to effectively managing relationships in organizations."

Nancy L. Southern, Ed.D
Saybrook Graduate School

"A handy summary of management and psychological theories and tools related to modern business organizations illustrated with views from leaders of successful corporations, and Jane's business and personal experiences and philosophy."

Richard A. Draeger, Vice President (ret.)
Pacific Gas and Electric Company

"This book is…A rapid-fire tour through management tools and techniques with an emphasis on human attributes as a resource; a brief overview of ideas and techniques to guide successful managers who understand people, teams and self; and, an upbeat review of ideas and methods guiding new or seasoned successful managers today."

Gibbe H. Parsons, MD,
Hospital Medical Director (past),
Professor of Medicine, Assistant Dean of CME,
University of California, Davis

"Although a slim volume, Ms. Macken's book offers a good survey of management and psychology concepts and principles for developing effective leadership and teams. The emphasis on self knowledge and continual self development is especially refreshing. The material covered in Ms. Macken's book is helpful to both new and experienced leaders – a quick introduction for new leaders and a reference guide for the experienced."

Fanny Lee, Director,
Business Requirements, PG&E

The Art of Managing…

How to Build a Better Workplace & Relationships

Jane Treber Macken, MBA, MA

ISBN 0-7414-3933-6

Published by:

INFI∞ITY
PUBLISHING.COM

1094 New DeHaven Street, Suite 100
West Conshohocken, PA 19428-2713
Info@buybooksontheweb.com
www.buybooksontheweb.com
Toll-free (877) BUY BOOK
Local Phone (610) 941-9999
Fax (610) 941-9959

Printed in the United States of America

Printed on Recycled Paper

Published April 2007

Contents

Acknowledgments

I want to acknowledge and thank those people in my life who have inspired this book: Terry Macken, my husband, who through his unconditional love has given me hope and courage to pursue my dream; Bill and Virginia Treber, my parents, who have always been my strongest advocates; Ron Lachini Jr., my son, through whose enthusiasm and adventurous spirit I gain energy; Tina Rohr, my daughter, who brings me back to the reality of the importance of relationships; Chuck Treber, my brother, who was my best friend growing up; Ken Dorking, the mentor who gave me my first opportunity to supervise; Dick Draeger, the mentor who encouraged me to earn my MBA; Susan Cohen, MFCC, therapist; Nancy Southern, Ed.D, adviser for MA-Organizational Psychology and counselor; Cathi "Cat" Wong, author's advocate and longtime friend; Julie "Cookie" Kaldveer, lifetime friend and confidant; Bev Cabellon, longtime friend; Melanie Rigney, the editor who made my work in this book shine; Jeniffer Thompson, Web site designer; and Penny Sansevieri, marketing expert.

Each of you has been instrumental in shaping me into the person I am today. I thank each of you with all my heart and soul.

Introduction

A very astute professor told me that we need to bridge the business world and the psychology world so that both people and business prosper and grow. The business world is about tasks and activities, and the psychology world is about getting to know ourselves, what motivates us, and how we interact with others. **Bridging business and psychology will assist you not only in managing your workplace, but also in managing your personal life. Both are really about successfully managing relationships.**

We all know people whom we admire. What is it about these people that garners admiration? Why do people respond favorably to these people? What is it that makes them successful both in their work lives and their personal lives? How did their environment and relationships impact who they are?

I have found through many years of working and supervising for a large corporation, managing a small business, continuing my education for over twenty-five years, and teaching several years at the graduate level that people who are successful possess three common attributes: caring and compassion for others, serving the community, and working on Self. These key attributes are responsible for building successful businesses, lasting relationships and a more balanced life.

This book bridges the worlds of business and psychology. It references the history of management theory, leadership, and organizational effectiveness; provides insights on how you can develop the characteristics of those who successfully manage both their workplace and their personal lives; and offers tools for forming effective teams and motivating people.

The names of people in this book have been changed to protect their identities.

Chapter 1: Understanding the History of Management Theory

To understand the three common themes to managing organizations and relationships, it is helpful to understand the history of management theory. This is important because as the needs of society and the environment change, history reflects the changing leadership and organizational needs of society. The progression and history of management theory provides the basis for this literature review.

Beginning in the 1760s, the Industrial Revolution moved the individual from the use of hand tools to the use of machinery for similar work. As businesses mechanized, there was a need to train unskilled workers on how to run the new equipment.

In 1776, Adam Smith advocated a system of projection based on employee specialization and economies of scale. Each employee concentrated on a particular part of a task, all of which were then put together to make a whole task. The business environment was relatively simple and straightforward—no unions; no complex labor negotiations; no local, state, or federal regulatory agencies. Managers in this era used a paternalistic style of management that resulted in the employees feeling loyalty toward the business because of job security.

As society moved into the 1850s, this era combined the merchant, craft, and guild organizations with a democratic free market that evolved into the modern industrial and manufacturing economy.

By early 1900s, Frederick Winslow Taylor brought forth a new concept called "scientific management" that broke down the job into component parts and measured results. He believed a single best method of organizing work could be discovered through a detailed study of the time and motion involved in doing each job. The principles of scientific management include: break jobs into their simplest parts; select the most suitable workers to fit the available jobs; turn those workers into specialists, each an expert in his own appointed task; arrange these specialized jobs along an assembly line; and design the right package of incentives, such as bonuses and prizes.

It was during this time that Abraham Maslow developed the "hierarchy of needs" theory as a model for managers to motivate their employees. The theory defines five levels of human needs:

Maslow's Hierarchy of Needs

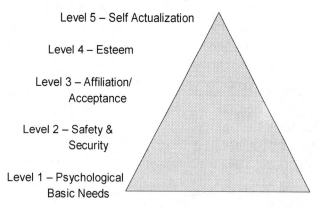

Level 5 – Self Actualization

Level 4 – Esteem

Level 3 – Affiliation/ Acceptance

Level 2 – Safety & Security

Level 1 – Psychological Basic Needs

Level 1—Psychological basic needs: food, water, clothing, shelter, sleep, sexual satisfaction

Level 2—Safety & Security—free from physical danger, loss of job or basics

Level 3—Affiliation/Acceptance: need to belong; acceptance by others

Level 4—Esteem: held in esteem by self and others (self confident, power, status)

Level 5—Self-Actualization: maximize one's potential and accomplish something

Maslow concluded that the previous level must be met before movement to the next level. I have found that you may go back to Level 1 or Level 2 because of life circumstances such as divorce, death, loss of job, or major disaster.

Then in 1916, Henri Fayol, referred to as "the father of modern management theory," divided industrial activities into six groups—technical, commercial, financial, security, accounting, and managerial. He developed fourteen principles that were used to teach management—division of work; authority and responsibility; discipline; unity of command; unity of direction; subordination of individual to general interest; remuneration; centralization; scalar chain; order; equity; stability of tenure; initiative; and esprit de corps. He also regarded the elements of management as functions of planning, organizing, commanding, coordinating, and controlling.

As businesses began to grow in the 1930s, there was a need for a different type of management. It was during this time that professional management evolved and was taught to managers at Alfred P. Sloan's graduate schools of business. These schools focused on the development of the general professional manager because managers now had to know the different functions of the business such as finance, marketing, design, and personnel. It was during this time that Henry Ford perfected the first "total quality management" (TQM) process by building assembly lines and splitting workers into different departments and functions such as marketing and design. Managers became generalists providing overall leadership for many functions and focusing on tasks.

It was during the 1950s and 1960s that the concept of humanistic management emerged, in which self-managing teams are created and workers are encouraged to suggest improvements. The human relations movement shifted theory from hard management to soft management. It was during this time that growth spurts in the size of business began. Since there were more people to manage, management development became a significant corporate function, with college recruitment programs, management trainee programs, programs to provide development transfer within the company, and internal and external training programs. It was during this era that management by objectives systems linked management processes, management development, and corporate business goals and objectives. Also during this period, the use of performance review systems emerged to monitor performance and determine compensation.

In 1957, Frederick Hertzberg developed theories of motivation in which he described certain "satisfiers" for motivation—achievement, challenging work, job growth, advancement, recognition, status, interpersonal relations, company policy, quality of supervision, security, working conditions, and salary.

Hertzberg's Theory of Motivation

Level 5 - Achievement
Challenging Work, Job Growth

Level 4 – Advancement,
Recognition, Status

Level 3 – Interpersonal
Relations, Company Policy

Level 2 – Quality of
Supervision, Security
Working Conditions

Level 1 - Salary

Hertzberg's Level 1—salary/ personal needs is comparable to Maslow's Level 1—psychological basic needs; Hertzberg's Level 2—quality of supervision/working conditions/job security is comparable to Maslow's Level 2—safety and security; Hertzberg's Level 3—interpersonal relations/company policy and administration is comparable to Maslow's Level 3—affiliation and acceptance; Hertzberg's Level 4—advancement/recognition/status is comparable to Maslow's Level 4—esteem (power/status/ self-confidence); and Hertzberg's Level 5—challenging work/achievement/growth in job responsibility is comparable to Maslow's Level 5—self-actualization. It was during this time that humanistic management began to focus on the needs of the individual.

Humanistic management brought about another theory of motivation. Douglas McGregor introduced Theory X and Theory Y assumptions about people. For example, Theory X suggested that people dislike work and will avoid it if they can. Theory Y suggests that the expenditure of physical and mental effort in work is as natural as play and rest. It was felt that managers must know how to communicate with and guide their employees so that they will see how they serve their own interests by working efficiently for an organization. Organizations continued to grow.

Motivation continued to be expanded. In 1964, Robert Blake and Jane Moulton developed the managerial grid that was used as a means of managerial training and of identifying various combinations of leadership styles. The focus was to balance the concern for production and the concern for people. In 1968, L. W. Porter and E. E. Lawler developed the model of motivation primarily for managers to link "effort" to "value of the reward." The performance was both intrinsic reward (sense of accomplishment or self-actualization) and extrinsic reward (working conditions and status).

During this time, David McClelland of Harvard University contributed to the motivation theory by identifying three types of basic motivating needs—power, affiliation, and achievement. People with the need for power have great concern for exercising influence and control. These people want the ability to induce or influence their beliefs or actions on other persons. People with the need for affiliation tend to derive pleasure from being loved and to avoid the pain of being rejected by a social group. These people are concerned with maintaining pleasant social relationships. People with the need for achievement have an intense desire for success and an equally intense fear of failure. Managers during this era generally scored high in achievement and power and low in affiliation.

In 1970, Fred E. Fiedler, a psychologist at the University of Illinois, suggested a contingency theory of leadership. He found that three critical dimensions of the leadership situation affected leadership—position power, task structure, and leader-member relations. In 1977, Robert Greenleaf, the longtime director of management and research at AT&T, stated that leadership is "situational" and rarely draws on known models. What was most inspiring is Greenleaf's concept that leaders are exceptional people from their own kind who consider themselves as "servants first," drawing on the individual's strengths. To this day, effective management is contingent or situational and this style still predominates today. In the early 1970s, the American economy experienced a recession as well as a change in the corporate attitude toward growth. After the recession, companies hired tremendous numbers of people, almost doubling their sizes. People took management positions for granted and enjoyed a secure lifetime of steadily rising affluence. Management theorists saw the 1970s as a time of flexible organizational structure and management processes within which the human elements that made up the organization could be conserved and utilized with greater flexibility and more efficiency.

This flexibility spawned matrix management in which the concepts that were taught in the 1970s were actually implemented in the 1980s. Alfred Sloan's modern multidivisional firm divided businesses into a set of semiautonomous operating units, each responsible for maintaining the market share and profits of a single business or market and each with division heads reporting to group headquarters in charge of setting long-term strategy and allocating capital. This was an era of decentralization and autonomy for the manager. However, even with decentralization, there was a rigid (and formal) command-and-control system.

In the 1980s, the American economy moved from the machine age into the information age, which included mobility of capital and managers facing the challenges of change and uncertainty in the areas of technology and intellectual knowledge. Tom Peters and Robert Waterman presented a study of business in their book *In Search of Excellence*." McKinsey & Company developed the McKinsey Model 7S management tool to analyze the elements of an organization for optimal effectiveness.

In 1987, Tom Peters preached "nuke hierarchy" and the need to learn to "thrive on chaos." He stated that successful management included four ingredients: "an uncanny sense of timing, an extraordinary ability to articulate the mood of the moment, the skill to dispense advice that sounds practical, and a talent for marketing." He stated that companies should shrink and get rid of middle managers, devolving power to the lowest level. Peters also stated that organizations must be flexible by reinventing themselves at the start of each day. His rationalistic model was financially performance-based, with little attention given to motivating workers or satisfying customers. The obsession with costs undervalued quality and value. Employees were treated as costs of production and liabilities rather than sources of value and assets. Peter's model encouraged bureaucratic conformity at the expense of entrepreneurial innovation. By contrast, today, managers know they must pay attention to the intuitive as well as the rational side of their jobs.

In the late 1980s, Peter Drucker focused on two themes—empowering workers and the rise of the "knowledge worker." He valued labor as a resource rather than just a cost. He believed that organizations are living.

During this time, there was a dramatic shift in management style. Managers through decentralization had autonomy, profit responsibility, and prestige within the organization and succeeded or failed almost without support from above. Managers were tough-minded and able to take pressure and stress. They focused on costs and efficiencies in productivity and quality.

It was during this time that W. Edwards Deming's "total quality management" (TQM) concept began to be used as a method to improve quality and productivity in most companies and government agencies. According to Deming, TQM fell short of creating transformational change because the focus was on statistical measurement rather than human interaction. His belief was that humans are born with intrinsic motivation—an inner drive to work and accomplish. He contended that many organizations blocked an individual's intrinsic motivation because of the bureaucratic paperwork, policies, and attitudes that discourage people from speaking openly. For these reasons, in the late 1980s and early 1990s, our culture went from detecting errors after the fact to one in which we prevented defects by improving the process. This program led to a reliance on figures and statistical analysis. It was during this time that technology began to enable a globally competitive environment.

Improving the managerial process that began in the 1980s and took hold in the late 1990s brought the emergence of matrix management, which was heavily participative and team oriented. In matrix management, companies organize around prudent grouping, such as finance, sales, and manufacturing. The formal structure organization had a multidimensional matrix. For example, individuals provided the work for one organization but reported to another organization. During this time, there was a traumatic shift from the loyalty-security tradeoff of the personally managed organization to the nonloyal, no-security organization. The shift felt dehumanizing to many workers. People were considered members of a team who were expendable if they did not perform. Policies and procedure stifled managers. The business units became scattered and diversified, and top execs may have sensed a loss of control over field operations. Each of these units competed for corporate resources and hoarded both technological and human resources. The bureaucratic systems that unified and coordinated companywide planning and control systems began to see proliferation of the systems and structures and controls of the large organization. People with financing backgrounds tended to rise to the top. With the increased use of teams, there was a shift emerging between the autocratic or bureaucratic style of leadership and the democratic or participative style of leadership. Motivational theories that demanded leaders of the old, traditional organization to have the need for power and achievement as their motivator now required the need for affiliation and achievement as the main motivators. This shift caused other studies of managerial styles needed for the new environment.

McBer and Company conducted a study during this time and developed a theory of six managerial styles for managing—coercive, authoritative, affiliative, democratic, pace-setting, and coaching. It is more commonly known as Ken Blanchard's and Paul Hersey's situational leadership model. Their studies found that no single managerial style is effective in all situations and with all people, and that leadership is dependent on the readiness of the follower.

In 1989, Warren Bennis's book *On Becoming a Leader* focused on how leadership differed from the traditional management style. Managers began to learn about leadership principles and that people tend to follow those whom they see as means of satisfying their own personal goals; and that the more managers understand what motivates their subordinates and understand how motivation operates, the more effective leaders they are likely to be.

In the 1990s, just as leaders were beginning to learn new principles, "The Age of Anxiety," a term coined by John Micklethwait and Adrian Woolridge emerged. They said: "The younger people who came into the labor market experienced the breakdown of the traditional American family; saw an increase in drugs, violence, and suicide; witnessed a steep decline in economic fortunes; and, had a general cynicism." This era included workers who were downsized, separated, unassigned, and proactively outplaced, including people who lost their jobs due to competition, technological change, and government budgets. Businesses were flattening hierarchies and empowering workers.

Additionally, corporations experienced contradictions: total quality management versus getting products and services faster to customers; corporate culture versus dealing with many cultures, beliefs, assumptions, and traditions; a single strong vision versus a changing environment due to the rapidly changing technology; global versus local; and shareholders versus stakeholders. The age of anxiety brings us into a new machine model.

James Champy and Michael Hammer introduced the concept of "reengineering." They advocated that business tear up old blueprints and completely redesign their organizations. They focused on the customer, who wants a quick answer and someone who will be responsible for it. Reengineering worked well on speed and service; managers were smashing down barriers with suppliers and competitors and forming alliances. Companies virtually turned themselves upside down (inverted pyramids) and encouraged worker democracy in the workplace.

According to James Champy and Michael Hammer, reengineering changes badly damaged morale because they evoked anxiety in the people who remained in the organizations. There was no more employee loyalty in these firms that reengineered. Trust levels plummeted. Reengineering adversely affected the innovation record of companies, including destroying the informal network of contacts that allow a product to gain acceptance within the organization.

However, reengineering works well in logistics and order fulfillment, because it forces a company to concentrate on speed and service—the two factors that most interest its customers. Modern companies are driven by their customers, not their bureaucracies.

Today, companies are cutting their corporate staff to the bone. They are focusing on core businesses and contracting out everything else. They are turning themselves into 'inverted pyramids," encouraging workplace democracy and handing power to front-line workers. Now, companies think about their stakeholders and how to increase their "well-being," not just profits.

In 1990, Peter Senge introduced the concept of "personal mastery," which is defined as people with a commitment to their own lifelong learning. In 1998, Navran Associates stated that an understanding of the essential human capacities provides a foundation for organizations to understand and integrate the skills, knowledge, habits, disciplines, principles, and practices that management theories provide. This results in genuine involvement, higher quality judgments and opinions, and a sense of shared vision for employees, customers, suppliers, and communities. Navran stated that gains from a learning organization are improved product and service, a decrease in wasted resources, a motivated workforce, increased profits, sustained competitive advantage, and better governmental and community relationships.

Companies now are taking a more "holistic" or "organic" approach to management theory. The next generation has emerged with better education and skills, including being raised to excel and achieve. This generation will come into the information age significantly contributing to the knowledge-value/based economy.

In the early 2000s, progressive companies are embracing "transformation," examining their businesses in the areas of operations, policy and strategy, project management, accounting and finance, and sales and marketing. Transformation embodies change management, performance improvement, performance measurement, process improvement, and reengineering. There is a deep fundamental assessment of every process and every organization. The culture is focused on teamwork and attempting to eliminate the silos that occurred in the 1980s. Some of the pressing issues are customer satisfaction and employee dissatisfaction. Customers expect more for less. Employees are disillusioned with management. Transformation has led to not only looking at processes, but also to valuing the employee.

Performance improvement focuses on benchmarking successful companies and their processes. Benchmarking has been a management tool since the 1980s. Performance management uses scorecards for key performance indicators. Process improvement is bringing back TQM to assist in organizational change and development. Reengineering in the 2000s is focusing on changing processes rather than fixing or placing constraints on processes.

In the 2000s, employees' values and beliefs are now a focus after years of neglect. Employees provide a product and/or service. **Managing the workplace is really about managing these relationships**.

Chapter 2: Organizational Effectiveness— The Competitive Edge

Management theory plays a key role in organizational effectiveness, which equates to not only staying in business but also being successful in business. Success is defined as being profitable and providing a product or service that people want and demand.

For a business to meet the demands of society, it must obtain a competitive edge in the market. Competition can erode a company's advantage, or share of the market, and reduce its profits. Competitive advantage comes through efficiency and effective management functions. For example, efficiency means improved processes such as the right staffing for the work, the right structure for specialization and integration, and quality work; effective management means the right style of leadership for the people, the alignment of core values of the company and people, the right skills for the tasks, and focus on the strategy. Effective and efficient management functions are important to the functioning of the organization.

In today's information age, competitive companies are driven by technology or produce technology. The emergence of technology in business in the past two decades threatens the traditional management process. Technology is changing the way people are managed. People can communicate using technology that enables spans of control to increase significantly from supervisor to more self-management.

With technology, organizations still need to exist. One of the most common methods to measure organizational effectiveness was developed by McKinsey & Company, an international management consulting firm. The McKinsey Model 7S is used to help clients make substantial and lasting performance improvements and build a firm that is able to attract, develop, excite, motivate, and retain exceptional people. The organizational elements include strategy, skills, shared values, staffing, systems, structure, and style.

Strategy refers to the way a company achieves a sustainable competitive advantage. Think three steps ahead of your competition while keeping the customer as the focus. The key is to find out what the customers want and give it to them. Successful alignment between the strategies and the people who do the work requires a great deal of communication to get people to understand and believe the vision and strategies. Theorists advise companies to come up with a strategic vision that provides a sense of mission without the costs and constraints of central planning. They suggest the company define a goal so resources can be organized and the workforce can be inspired to pursue this common goal. **Successful strategy helps the company be profitable. Profit is like breathing—you are not healthy unless you are making a profit.**

Skills refer to the basic competencies of the company and its people. A company must either be competent in its business or form alliances, partnerships, and/or joint ventures to ensure competency. Skill attributes include intelligence, technical expertise, education, project management, leadership, and teamwork. Intelligence is the ability to integrate reason and intuition. Technical expertise is the technological capabilities. Education is upgrading skills for the individual, demands of the market and latest technologies. Project management is an integrated environment to manage projects, tasks, issues and resources. Leadership is how we draw on our own values and capabilities to plan, lead, organize and motivate others. Teamwork is a solution for managing work and communication through projects. It is important to identify skills gaps for each of your employees. When these skill gaps are identified, the employee must grow to narrow and eliminate the gap by attending educational and training courses. Think of this as a ship. As the ship moves forward, you must upgrade your skills to remain on board. If you don't upgrade your skills, you will fall off the ship. People who are interested in learning and can transfer knowledge are the best source of intellectual capital. Organizations, large or small, learn only through individuals who learn. Employ the best skilled people who are intelligent and educated and can apply knowledge. **People who continue to work on themselves—behavior modification, relationships, and technical skills—not only are better team workers, but also have the capacity and desire to think "out of the box."**

Shared values, more commonly known as core values, refers to the guiding concepts and dominant values, beliefs, and assumptions. The attributes identified with shared values are trust, integrity/truthful, accountability, relationships, continuous learning, risk taking and valuing diversity. Trust means keeping confidences. Rumors, gossip, and unauthorized sharing of personal and embarrassing information violate the confidences and show disrespect for others. Integrity/truthful is telling the truth. The only exception is when someone asks how his or her new outfit looks. The person is really only looking for validation of the purchase, not necessarily the truth. Adultery is unethical because it dishonors the promise made on one's wedding day—to be faithful to one's spouse. Once trust has been broken, it is hard if not impossible to restore it fully. Keeping your promises builds trust and loyalty in relationships. Accountability is really about keeping your promises. You are expected to do what you say you are going to do. Continuous learning is necessary in a diverse culture. Being well read and traveling both assist in understanding other cultures and acceptance for each person's uniqueness and individuality. Diversity is an absolute necessity because it generates more ideas resulting in greater creativity and innovation. Risk taking includes empowerment, creativity, and innovation. Bill Gates once said that people who have worked at companies that failed have a lot of good experiences in thinking through tradeoffs and that success is a lousy teacher. **The congruence between individual values and organizational values results in the company's continued growth and profitability**.

Staffing refers to the company's approach to human resources management, including recruitment, motivation, and retention. Organizations want people who are committed to working hard and getting results. Staffing continues to be a concern because there is a shortage of knowledge-valued people and high turnover. There has been a paradigm shift from long-term employment to short-term employment. Staffing is the art of hiring the right people. If people care and are doing what they want to do, they are genuinely committed and are full of energy and enthusiasm. **The right staffing produces the right results.**

Systems are the formal procedures that support strategy and structure, including information systems, performance measurement and reward systems, and budgeting and control systems. They are the formal methods to support and achieve strategies, goals, and objectives. Systems are more powerful than they are generally given credit for. **Well-defined systems give people the freedom to act, try out their own ideas, and be responsible for achieving results.** Use systems to attain success: Measures or metrics track and monitor progress; human resources systems reward results; and information systems gather data, monitor productivity, and communicate information to all. Control systems are effective measuring systems that monitor production and delivery schedules and reward teams and individuals for achieving the goals and objectives.

Structure refers to the primary basis for specialization and integration, influenced by strategies and the organization's size and diversity. Organizations that have a flexible structure can continually shift to fit or anticipate market and business climate changes. A key theme is **"in order for you to succeed, others must succeed as well."**

For example, here are several types of structures that are suggested for the described situations.

Situation	Type of Structure
When efficiency and depth of knowledge or skill are critical.	**Functional** *(Separate Departments for Marketing, Human Resources, Finance, Operating)*
When the adaptability to environmental contingencies and decentralized decision making are required.	**Divisional/Product** *(From Design Concept to Product)*
When the need is to focus on the customer versus broader environmental contingencies.	**Geographical/Customer Location**
When the need is for adopting complex organizational structure for greater flexibility. Can have multiple functional managers.	**Matrix** *(Cross-Functional)*
When the need is for integration and coordination across functions and processes in response to rapid changes in customer needs and demands for value.	**Horizontal/Team Based** *(Functions and Process Oriented)*
When the need is for flexibility to build on advantages of different approaches and compensate for weaknesses.	**Hybrid** *(Variety of Strategic Needs)*

The structure that matters is one that gives customers what they want and identifies someone who can be held accountable and responsible for that.

Style is the leadership and management method. Style is what leaders and managers do more than what they say, how they spend their time, and what they focus attention on. Style includes management philosophy and the way people lead and manage the company and relationships. It is one of the most critical organizational components. Successful people lead by example and have high expectations for themselves and others. They do what's right for the organization, then what's right for the team, and lastly what's right for the individual. **The best leadership style is one that has a clear personal vision, focused energies, developed patience, an objective view of reality, a connection to others and life itself, and a desire for continued learning.**

By understanding the strengths and weaknesses of each of these organizational components, the business can define its future threats and opportunities for strategic planning.

When analyzing the characteristics and attributes of successful companies, general themes of the learning organization emerge: successful leaders promote thinking and acting at all levels by teaching decision making through example; the process of learning is as important as what the employee learns; innovation and creative thinking are practiced; the smartest people know how to learn from mistakes; collaborative management teams can produce powerful results; leaders aspire to serve; and leaders' possible future and success depend on the ability to see and respond to a wide variety of alternatives.

There is a paradigm shift in America's future from rewards based on individual performance to rewards based on company and team performance, and from blame and excuses to personal accountability, such as understanding that you and the cause of your problem are part of a single system.

Knowledge is the new source of power and wealth. Leadership style is the most valued characteristic for organizational effectiveness and knowledge development. The most significant contribution leaders can make is the long-term development of people who adapt, prosper, and grow. People have the ability to continuously learn. People can be taught how to work effectively in groups. It's important for leaders to understand how they themselves think and react so that they can begin to understand how others might think and react. The style of leaders can make a difference.

Three common themes are important for effective leaders in the twenty-first century. Leaders must have caring and compassion for people, serve others and the community, and continue the development of Self. **People who continue to learn are better able to implement and manage continuous change, meet customer expectations and needs, and lead an organization to success in the competitive economic environment.**

Chapter 3: Environment and Relationships Impact Who We Are

Before I talk about the three themes for managing organizations and relationships—caring and compassion for people, serving others and the community, and developing Self—I want to talk about our environment and how the relationships in our life affect who we are today.

Up until we begin school, our families have the biggest influence on our lives. Our basic personalities are formed by the age of three, and we develop into little human beings by the age of six. Once we begin school, teachers and friends begin to influence our behavior. It's amazing how others believe that they see what we should or should not do with our life better than we who actually planned our life's lessons. Each of us goes through life fulfilling our dreams and other's expectations. It is our dreams that bring us the most rewarding experiences. Think back in your life when you were happiest…it was when you were fulfilling your dream.

My happiest moment when I was young was in my junior year when I tried out for head song girl for Washington High School's football season the following year. I worked so hard learning the routine. My best friend worked with me since she had been a previous head song girl. After the tryouts, they announced the six song girls, starting with the sixth person and working up to the head song girl. When they had announced five, I began to softly cry. I knew I had not made the group. I felt devastated. So, when they called my name for head song girl, I didn't hear it. My friend began pushing my shoulder and others started calling my name. It was then that I realized what was happening. I was so embarrassed, and so excited! I jumped up and went onto the stage where we all did the routine for the audience.

A child's base personality is formed during the first three years of life. Whether the child was planned or unplanned affects how the child is folded into the family. I was a planned child and reared by my mother and father. They loved one another, but I sensed that they had a dysfunctional marriage. My dad was an alcoholic and my mother was a rage-aholic. These behaviors result in the "pleaser" and "acting out" type of behaviors in the children. I was the former and my brother was the latter. As a "pleaser," I continuously had to prove my worth and would not let myself fail. I have observed a tremendous number of women in management who were "pleasers" and who had a fear of failure. Understanding the lives of your parents helps with your self-development.

For example, as a daughter of an alcoholic father and grandfathers, I was codependent. Codependency is defined as the lack of Self or ego development. Usually, it involves strong negative programming against anger, wants, and beliefs. People who are codependent look to external validation for self-worth. It's about living from the outside in, molding oneself to fit around others' lives instead of directing the course of one's own life from internal cues, hopes, dreams, wisdom, and power.

As I grew from childhood and adolescence into adulthood, my parents were not able to consistently attend to my needs, were not able to help me believe that I was special, and were not able to offer me a sense of emotional safety. My home was devoid of showing feelings. There was little if any praising, encouraging, and giving of physical affection. I experienced the parent-child dyad in which I was pitted against my mother, resulting in emotional and psychological abuse. Our family had rigid rules and unrealistic expectations and inappropriate disciplining techniques. Little time was given to my brother and me.

I had problems as an adult. I found that I did not feel good about myself, had difficulty trusting people, was unable to identify my needs and allow them to be met. During the summer of 1991, I felt as if my whole world was collapsing. I found that I had great difficulty in my ability to get close to others, which created problems in my personal and professional life. During this time, my family members and I could not communicate without anger. I was in a second-level management position and my employees banded together to tell me what they did not like about my leadership style—inflexibility and lack of compassion or caring for others.

I had a great fear of rejection by my family members and work associates. I wanted to please everyone. The more I tried, the worse things got. I had worked hard and accomplished much during the past twenty years, not only raising two children but also continuing my education in an effort to win the approval of my family, friends, and coworkers.

I began working on Self. I began psychotherapy for the primary goal of coping with anxiety, anger, confusion, and a diminished sense of well-being with a secondary goal of modifying my behaviors and working toward becoming an empathic and compassionate person. On the surface I appeared self-sufficient and self-actualized, but I was truly depressed and suffered deep emotional pain. I was hard driving, workaholic, self-righteous, enabling, controlling, and in denial. Do you know people like this? You may see these characteristics in first-level supervisors and mid-level managers. By working on Self, these people will be able to have more caring and compassion for others.

Today, I am in touch with my feelings. I have compassion for my parents because they raised my brother and me within their own limitations of significant trauma in their lives, both financial and emotional.

I mentioned that I was a workaholic. What I have found is that everyone has an addiction, whether it is alcohol, food, work, working out, or something else. Sometime in our life we realize that we are addicted to something, so we stop. What happens is that we trade that behavior for another behavior and become addicted to something else. For example, if we are addicted to food, once we get eating under control, we may become addicted to working out. Of course, if it's beneficial to your mind, body, and spirit, it's more acceptable to both you and society.

I have also found that everyone is obsessive and compulsive about something. It's when it takes over your everyday life that it becomes a disorder, commonly known as OCD. Have you known anyone who is always dieting? I am compulsive about my weight; however, I know that my image of how I look is not the same as others see me. Therefore, I use the scale as my sanity check. I usually will stay within five pounds. When someone gets too thin or obese, or purges/binges, he/she then has an eating disorder. Have you known anyone who would not allow you to bring coffee into a meeting room, only water? Have you known anyone who is very neat and has everything in its place? Have you known anyone who has a really clean house or automobile? Have you known someone who washes the hands very frequently? Have you known anyone who is extremely meticulous of how he/she is groomed? What I am trying to say is that we are all obsessive and compulsive to some degree. It is only when any of our behaviors are carried to the extreme that it can be a disorder. This is part of understanding yourself.

The environment and relationships impact our life. Those people who influenced me most pushed me in the direction of continuous education. My deep yearning for knowledge actually made the learning happen. During my life, I obtained several degrees. As a first-line supervisor, I obtained a bachelor's degree in management degree in 1986. As an administrative assistant to a vice president and second-level supervision, I obtained an MBA degree in 1991. For self-development, I took general psychology courses and obtained a master's in organizational psychology degree in

1998. As an adjunct faculty member for a university, I taught managing organizations and organizational structure from 1999 to 2002. Working for my husband's business, I obtained public notary and real estate broker licenses in 2005 and 2006, respectively. What I have found is that the more I learn, the more I realize how much I don't know. I truly believe that continuing education and building on skills is the key to a successful life that can be shared with others.

Our environment and relationships impact who we are and what we do. Based on my early experiences, I am a high achiever and codependent, which means that I continually strive to be better and put others' needs ahead of my own. However, I now choose what and when I put someone else's needs before my own. It is my dream that this book can help you achieve your goals and dreams. It is with this thought that I want to share what I learned about the three common themes to managing organizations and relationships.

Chapter 4: Caring & Compassion for People

I completed a master's thesis on "Personal Mastery in Organizational Leadership" in 1998. I interviewed seven industry leaders. One of the common themes that emerged was the fact that successful leaders demonstrate caring and compassion for people. They show deep sympathy and empathy, which is an intellectual or emotional identification with another; mutual understanding or affection; ability to share another's ideas, emotions; to feel concerned about or interested in another.

Personal mastery is defined as knowing who I am, how I come to believe what I believe, knowing me really well and how I filter things in the world. Try working to bridge the gap between your own perception of Self and others' perception of you.

Have you seen someone who has "attitude"? You may want to say something to the person. Some people act this way to balance the power dynamic; others do not even know how they are coming across to others. They may be hostile because they are short or because they learned that personal style in their culture. For example, when someone comes to California from New York, there is a culture difference. The New York style can be construed as directness and sometimes aggressiveness. I had the opportunity to work with a woman from New York. When I told her I struggled with how direct she was because sometimes it came out as abrasive, she became upset. She was unaware of how others perceived her directness.

Personal mastery is a willingness to know me...really well. When I know me really well, then personal power is inevitable and is the real difference in control. Either you are controlling yourself or others are controlling you. CEOs do not believe they are as great as others see them, and they typically are in control of themselves.

Personal mastery is a lifelong journey of bridging the gap between who I think I am and who others think I am. To bridge this gap, ask questions and dialogue beginning with these words: what, how, tell me why. Once you get better understanding of how others perceive you, the gap will get smaller, resulting in learning how to communicate and work well together.

To help define the gap, businesses use the 360-degree feedback survey that is a multi-rater assessment tool. The tool is a proven method to gathering important information on how behaviors are perceived in the workplace. This tool can be used for leadership development, performance assessment and improvement, team building, career development, succession planning, and training needs assessment.

We judge others by their behavior, but we judge ourselves by our intentions. To close the gap, we must be open to change and suggestions. If you are unable to explore and be tied into your job as who you are, you are considered a learning disability. An example of dialogue can be analyzed by use of the Johari window.

Johari Window
Analysis of Dialogue

OPEN

BLIND

Known to You   Known to Me

Known About Others   Unknown to Self

HIDDEN

UNKNOWN

Known to Me   Unknown by You

Unknown by Me   Unknown by You

Open communication is something that is known to both you and me. Hidden is something known by me and unknown by you. Blind is something that is unknown to me and known by you. Unknown is something that neither of us knows.

If I share something with you about me, I build a relationship. The sense of honesty bridges and builds relationships. Our shadow fears dishonesty in Self. Our shadow is our hidden potential. For example, think of a toy box. In the toy box are all the negative things people said to you or things you are ashamed of, your secrets. From the earliest time that you can remember, someone told you not to do or say something that made you feel ashamed and/or guilty. You put that behavior, thought, or word into the toy box. Years of stuffing this toy box with all the things we are ashamed of or someone told you not to do or say results in emotional reactions to others. When someone says or does something, we sometimes respond lovingly; other times, our feelings get hurt or we become sad or afraid or feel guilty. So, we go into a mode of "fight or flight"—anger, rage or withdrawal and cutoff all emotional and verbal communication.

When you react emotionally to something someone said or did, it is usually a reaction to something from your past. You are getting your stuff into the current situation. It's your shadow, the part of you that is hidden in the toy box. Some people act out toward another person, others keep it inside. Reflect to see where it's coming from. **People can only evoke reactions in us if we choose to let them**. By reflecting and going back in time to when you first remember a similar work, situation, person, or incident, you can work through the original incident and replace it with what it should have been to make you feel OK. By replacing negative messages with positive messages, you can overcome negative programming, which then allows you to respond to others rather than react. As you react less to your environment, you will gain an inner peacefulness and be more in harmony with your relationships and your environment. The result is a more caring and compassionate person.

It takes a lifetime of working on these emotional reactions to rid yourself of your shadow. These are the blind spots we all face. As you work on emotional reactions, a key skill is to develop advocacy and inquiry techniques. These techniques are simply asking questions that begin with "What, who, how, tell me why or describe." There is a paradigm shift from men being rewarded for advocacy and women for inquiry; now, both men and women are rewarded for both advocacy and inquiry.

To improve advocacy, ask, "Here is what I think and here's how I got there." This comment explains your assumptions and describes the information that led to them. A question you could ask is, "What do you think about what I just said?" This question encourages others to explore your assumptions and information. Refrain from defensiveness when your ideas are questioned.

To improve inquiry, ask questions: "What leads you to conclude that?" "What causes you to say that?" "What do you mean?" "How did you arrive at this view?" "Have you considered…?" **What, how, and tell me why are nonaggressive inquiry words that allow better understanding and eliminate defensiveness**.

Successful business relationships are built on honesty and emotional maturity. By developing good advocacy and inquiry skills and making progress on understanding and working on eliminating your shadow, your behaviors become more compassionate toward others. Personal mastery is not only working on Self, but also a willingness to get to know me.

The leaders I interviewed show patience and connectedness to others, including expecting no more or no less from others than they were willing to do, controlling their emotions by seeing the situation from others' point of view, trusting others, being trustworthy, and being raised to treat people kindly and with humanity.

The leaders also demonstrated qualities of trusting; setting high expectations; caring for people; focusing on being open and meeting people's unique needs; displaying a sense of fairness; using humor and vulnerability; being honest; having a strong value system; being personally involved; having a good sense of Self; and modeling behavior they wanted others to follow. For example, one leader said, "Being able to express caring and trust toward others is rewarding and recognized by others who respond in like...People trust me because I trust them. I believe in their commitment and intelligence and ability to deliver." Another said, "People tell me I'm incredibly patient...I like people...I've always liked people."

Successful leaders demonstrate trust, integrity, and credibility, including leading by example, making people feel and believe that everybody is equally important and that everything they do is significant. For example, one leader interviewed said, "Everything is significant, so don't belittle or diminish anyone's contribution."

Leaders who have developed a deep caring for people are usually influenced by either parental role models and/or mentors. These role models genuinely care for people and treat them kindly and respectfully. For example, one leader said, "I guess I'd have to say my parents" when asked for his role models. After a pause, he said, "I was raised to respect everyone...to care for everyone." Another leader said, "Of course, this is just the way that you were raised and the values that your family and church put on you." These leaders respect and recognize the individual's dignity.

Another critical part of caring is controlling emotions. Successful leaders are able to respond rather than react emotionally in emotionally charged situations. For example, several of those interviewed said that they developed patience early in life because losing one's temper was not acceptable.

Others are able to step back and listen for understanding and assess what's really going on. For example, one leader said, "The first thing that I've done is to always try to anticipate that if I were in the other person's position why would I be behaving that way." After a pause, he said, "Rational people make rational decisions…when people make irrational decisions, there is usually a reason or cause or events that are overwhelming them. I try to spend time to listen and understand what that is, because most of the time, there are ways you can pull the person back away from the emotional side of their position, so they can make rational decisions." He then said, "People's hidden and conflicting agendas sometimes cause behavior that you don't want." Leaders' patience leads to their ability to communicate effectively by forming honest relationships of trust and credibility.

In 1997, Max DePree, who is a leading organizational management theorist with forty years of corporate experience, stated that success as human beings requires competence in relationships. Successful leaders help people move toward their potential and service by looking for the unique talents of people, accepting human authenticity, and giving people the opportunity to learn and grow.

Each person is a unique individual. Accepting others requires no racial or sexual stereotyping. Racial and sexual stereotyping and casual put-downs are so demeaning that it's hard to believe that the person saying these things really means it. Put-downs disrespect us as well as others. Our competitive nature keeps us jockeying for position, measuring where we stand, and assumes there is only a limited amount of rightness in the world. For a relationship whether at work or home, we must be self-respectful as well as respectful of one another. Caring is recognizing each other's full and individual humanity.

It's true that the more information we have about the world, the more clearly we understand what we don't know. It is also true that we don't need to learn anything at all in order to deal fairly with others and to walk gently in the world. The wisdom that we need is inside us. Instinct tells us how to treat others because we know how we want others to treat us, and we know that all people are one.

According to Nancy Southern, Ed.D, communicative competence happens when the principles of comprehensibility (understanding), shared values (compassion, caring), truthfulness, and trust are met. By respecting another point of view, we create an opportunity for shared learning and authentic relationship which expresses genuine caring for others and life itself.

Forming honest relationships is important for successful leadership because a good leader must have help from others. Leaders can only lead successfully through caring and compassion for others.

Chapter 5: Serving Others and the Community

The second common theme that emerged from successful leaders relates to serving others and the community by being a role model for others to emulate and by teaching others.

As an adjunct faculty member at a San Francisco Bay Area university, I taught Peter Senge's Fifth Discipline concepts that embraced systems thinking, that aligns well with serving others and the community. I would ask the students, "When you think of systems thinking, is the whole system the members of this class? Or is it the students and faculty at this university? Or, does it involve this city and the community?" These questions led to much dialogue. If we are really looking at the system, the question is, "What impact do I have on what?"

The system could include the universe, or it could be just a small group in an organization. Rather than acting as an individual, you might act in concert with a group. If questions or concerns come up around a big issue, how does the group narrow the issue down to address the underlying problem? Let's say a couple is getting divorced. The reason is not because he left his socks on the floor or she left the dirty dishes in the sink. People don't get divorced because of these issues. These are only symptoms and symbolize the system of disrespect, different styles, and different values. In an organization, excessive sick leave, injuries, low productivity, and low morale are symptoms and symbolize lack of leadership.

The system is sometimes larger than we can handle, so when doing systems thinking, it is important to know how and what we do impacts the whole system. It is communicating to find out how we affect other areas and other people's work or lives.

Systems thinking is looking at the whole system and understanding the big picture. In the 1970s, organizations fostered silo thinking. Operations, human resources, marketing, information technology, and finance all operated as line departments and did not talk to one another. These departments actually competed for resources and rewards. In today's environment, transformation is breaking down and closing these silos by creating open dialogue and communications.

The word *dialogue* comes from the Greek word dialogos, which is from dia and a tense of legein, to speak, according to Merriam-Webster's Unabridged. Dia means through and Logue means meaning. Therefore, dialogue means moving through. The key to dialogue is listening. When listening, go beyond the words and get to the meaning of what someone is trying to say. Listening is definitely an art. Try listening from within the other person's life.

Being a true participant in authentic dialogue is an invaluable skill. We learn to speak *from* experience and to listen *for* experience. By sharing and risking the truth of our experience, we discover important questions that can guide our interpretations of contexts, of others, of ourselves. Dialogue is two-way communication between the sender and receiver. The sender talks from experiences and beliefs and the receiver listens and decodes for experiences and beliefs.

Open dialogue is the ability to speak and be heard without judgment and interruption as well as the ability to watch others and be aware of how they receive. Each person must be given the space to express beliefs and ideas without having to defend them. How many times have you started to say something and the other person interrupted you before you finished? I know I catch myself doing this occasionally. I have also experienced others doing it to me. Do you remember how you felt not being able to complete your thought? And, on top of that, perhaps you even forgot the point that you were trying to make. Or, perhaps you just clammed up because you decided maybe the other person really couldn't care less about what you were saying. You may have felt a sense of anger, sense of helplessness, sense of confusion and frustration. What happens? People stop communicating. **Listen to what is not said. Implied is often more important than spoken**. Think between sentences. Digest what is said and not said before engaging your mouth. Watch your prejudices. Prejudice will distort what you hear, so listen without prejudging.

Conversely, when you are speaking, observe how your behavior and your words are being received by the person or people you are speaking to. For example, use of "I" or "We" messages help reduce anger and confrontation. Using "You" immediately puts the other person on the defensive, which leads to anger, withdrawal, or other personal defense mechanisms. A good example is a situation where a customer calls or comes into the office expressing anger and is visibly upset. A reaction would be to match the person's anger (by getting angry yourself) or avoidance (pretending the other person isn't angry) of the person's emotional state. A response showing caring and understanding would be, "I understand your concern. How can we work this out or what would it take to correct this situation?" Another example would be if a friend or family member said something that you did not understand. A reaction would be, "You're not being clear." A response would be, "I don't understand." Watching others' reactions can give you valuable information.

Communicating and working together effectively allows people to get to know each other. Once you've gotten to know someone, it's much easier to work with him/her. Once you've established a relationship, you work better because you treat each other as a person. How people think about their work and how they feel about relationships they maintain at work and the company itself all have significant impacts on their behavior choices and ultimately on the performance of the organization.

In business, the advantages of dialogue are increased employee satisfaction and commitment, lower turnover, and increased innovation and flexibility. The limitation is that dialogue is time consuming.

Effective dialogue has an impact on systems thinking concept because for any one member to succeed, all must succeed. Successful leaders are effective communicators who use dialogue successfully to serve others and the community.

In the workplace, you see very smart people who never actually "make it" in supervision or management. Often, the reason is that even with all their knowledge, they cannot relate to other people, including motivating others and getting them on their side. They do not possess the sense of community, the caring and compassion for others.

It takes courage and acceptance of the knowledge that our responsibility in this life is to our own healthy development and not to controlling someone else's development. The key is to let other people grow, develop, and live their own experiences. Our need to control someone else generally results from our own insecurities. Because we lack the understanding of our own personal worth, we look for it in someone else's devotion to us.

I have observed that folks who were raised in small towns and/or large families usually have a great sense of community. In these situations, everyone knows everyone's business and there are few secrets, and when you need help and support, the community/family is there for you. These trusting relationships carry over into these people's adult lives and often result in demonstrative, genuine caring and compassion for others. People like working with and for these types of people.

Even if you did not have the opportunity to be raised in a small town or a large family, you can learn these skills through community involvement and mentorship. For example, you can donate time to a community project (Junior Achievement, Adopt-A-Highway, Run for Cancer, etc.), make an honest effort to bond with others by being open and honest in everything that you do, and find someone who has these skills to act as your mentor. A mentor can help you by pointing out behaviors that help you develop this skill as well as behaviors that get in the way of developing this skill. For example, a good mentor is someone who has a good sense of community and shows caring and compassion for others. This person will not be afraid to be candid with you and will not simply tell you what you want to hear. Good mentors will be honest and open because they want you to succeed.

Folks who do not have these skills may not be truthful and honest because their internal dialogue is saying "He won't like me" or "I am afraid of retaliation." These types of people come from fear-based thinking that brings about dishonesty and lying. In their minds, they are not actually lying; what they are saying is their truth because of the fear they might feel if they were to tell the truth. It is only when folks are truthful and honest that they can build and maintain successful organizational relationships.

Organizations want to build successful leaders and collaborative teams to enhance existing processes or develop new processes. Leaders and team members who have a sense of community, caring, and compassion for others function fully. They are aware that for success, all must succeed. You are only as good as your weakest member. Successful people serve and teach others.

Because we learn from each other, we must rid the old style of "I'm right." For example, the procedures manual indicates that you do something in a specific way. Someone else wants to do something in a way counter to the manual. Since you believe the manual is right, you say, "I don't have to listen to you; you are wrong." What would happen if you said, "You have a good idea and maybe the manual needs to address your idea?" This comment would not only open communication and dialogue, but it also would promote learning.

You may want to look at the experience of a toddler. A child learns by trying. We often tell the toddler the right and wrong things they should or shouldn't do, but no one says it's a bad idea. Then in first grade, someone tells the child to become responsible and that A's are better than F's. Learning becomes painful. We learn from others by collaborating because we do not have all the answers (even though some times we believe we do).

Collaboration requires dialogue. Group projects where teamwork is required produce two results—the actual product and the ability to put aside one's own assumptions and beliefs and become aware of other people's realities. Everyone comes to the table with an opinion, and every opinion will be different and every opinion is valid.

For my dissertation, I interviewed several successful industry leaders who supported the theory of serving others by incorporating each team member's personal vision with their vision. They described how they develop a clear personal vision and focus their energies toward that vision. Each one of them took time to reflect, contemplate, or dream of where they wanted to be and where they needed to take others, whether personal, family, company, or community.

"Instilling what I tend to see...I let this stuff percolate up until a vision comes to me," one leader said.

Another said: With respect to my personal vision, I immediately focus in on "what's the headline...and what are the top three headlines?"...For my business, I focus on where I'm trying to be a year from now; where do I want to be in three years from now, five years, even ten...and sort of peel the onion back to get whatever the detail is so I can create a road map for others to follow...By getting people to focus on that (headline)—boy, does that get everything driving toward congruence.

I find that the use of the word "headliner" builds a mental picture that keeps people focused on what's happening and on where leaders need to focus their energy.

The gift of caring for others is taught early in life; however, this is a skill that can be learned at any age. Even though we tend to do as our parents did or as someone we looked up to and modeled did, we can change our behaviors if challenged and taught.

Another leader stated, "You coach individuals, provide feedback, identify their skills gaps, and then move forward...coaching...helping others reach their potential." I truly believe there was a genuine feeling of the people interviewed of wanting to help others reach their potential, including identifying areas for others to work on so that they can improve.

One of the leaders said:

"I encourage leaders in my organization...by example, not just by directive—to engage in some leadership role in the community—service or charity of their choice. It causes some people on the team to spend some of their time in community service...I find that that causes people to be more positive and think of themselves as showing some leadership...it's great for the attitude, it's great for the spirit...and (service to the community) causes people to have a little bit more balance in their lives."

Successful leaders feel a connection to others and life itself, which is one of the elements of personal mastery. They also demonstrate two additional elements: the ability to have a clear personal vision and focused energies to achieve that vision by serving the needs of others, including the business and community. I believe that by reaching out to others, we not only help them in their need, but also meet our own individual needs of affiliation, achievement, and power.

It's a continuous circle of giving and receiving—the more you give the more you get.

A quote from *Tao Te Ching* by Stephen Mitchell says it best:

"The more he does for others...the happier he is: Because he is doing it for himself. The more he gives to others, the wealthier he is: Because the less you hold on to, the more you can give yourself to others. When you give yourself completely, your wealth is infinite."

Chapter 6: Developing of Self

The third common theme is the development of Self. Continue to develop Self because people are expected to grow. To develop Self, work on the mind though continuous learning, the body though exercise and proper nutrition and the spirit through quiet time such as meditation, contemplation, reflection or relaxation. Quiet time helps you define where you are, where you want to go and what you must do to get there.

The development of Self theme emerged from my interviews with successful leaders and means to uncover personal growth and awareness in relation to the individual, the business, and the community. I believe the economy and knowledge-based individuals require leaders to continue personal growth. When people are striving to improve Self, they are more open to learning and more energized by opportunities to learn. The individual and the organization interact with congruence. The payoffs can be increased commitment, higher levels of energy and enthusiasm, sincere dedication to success of the group, and a general positive effect on many people's lives. By setting challenging goals for ourselves, we can expect to develop the drive and ambition to move forward in our lives. **As we develop Self, we will have a better understanding of creating the lives that we most desire for ourselves.**

What I mean by working on Self includes:

- know Self (through therapy, counseling, or personal growth groups to learn about strengths and weaknesses to manage biases and weaknesses)

- attend professional meetings (to benchmark other practices with what you are doing)

- give presentations (to check your Self and hold your work up to scrutiny)

- solicit feedback and evaluation (from clients, peers, external partners, and family to gain perspective on where you are)

- practice spirituality (daily time to meditate about work, role, and outcomes, including questioning intentions and integrity)

- be honest with yourself and clients (acknowledging when not neutral in your beliefs, labeling biases and admitting your own agenda)

Understanding yourself includes understanding your emotions (fear, anger, sadness, guilt, rage, shame, happiness, joy). When you feel an emotion, reflect to see where it is coming from. **People can only evoke reactions in us if we choose to let them.** By reflecting and going back in time to when you first remember a similar word, situation, person, or incident, you can work through the original incident by replacing those memories with what should have been to make you feel OK. By replacing negative messages with positive ones, we overcome negative programming and become more in harmony with our relationships and our environment. As you begin to understand yourself more and more, you will respond positively to more and more situations and relationships with understanding and compassion.

In 1997, I completed a study on the characteristics and attributes of successful companies that doubled their sales every four years—Applied Materials, Atmel Corporation, Chiron Corporation, Cisco Systems, Foundation Health, Hewlett-Packard, Infinity Financial, Microsoft, The Money Store, Silicon Graphics, Solectron, and S3. Their size ranged from 250 employees to 300,000 employees. I wanted to explore the link between high levels of personal mastery and leadership. I interviewed CEOs, vice presidents, chairmen, general managers, and managers with twenty to forty-five years of experience each.

Those leaders interviewed had a good understanding of Self and exhibited the attributes of those people who clearly work on Self. They had a special sense of purpose. They saw their current reality as an opportunity, welcomed change, felt connected to others and life itself, believed they influenced others, enjoyed their journey and exuded confidence even though they were aware of their weaknesses.

When asked how she developed Self, one leader stated, "The way you look at life and why you are put here on earth...listen to people, read and continue to learn." Another stated, "I think it's a philosophy that I have, particularly in relationship complexity. I was brought up reaching out and caring for people...personal mentoring...and, making sure that the learning and feedback help with development." Another leader said: "I think I had the fortune of working for people who probably exhibit these characteristics early in my career and people who I thought had particular skills or manners that I felt would be effective for me."

I believe that even if you do not have a parental role model, you can learn from any mentor or model of this behavior. The importance is to create an environment in the workplace with the right leadership.

These attributes can be applied to not only individuals but also to organizations. Whether a person, a family, or a billion-dollar company, where there is a will to make it happen and an understanding about how to do so, success is likely to follow.

Leaders must be vulnerable to their followers. According to Peter Senge, leaders' vulnerability is the essence of developed patience and seeing reality objectively. Successful leaders are better able to manage their internal objectivity by:

- knowing themselves (personal growth)

- benchmarking against others to see how they are doing

- soliciting feedback from peers and colleagues

- giving presentations to gain critical review for their work

- incorporating spiritual practice (quiet reflection, meditation, or contemplation) to review where they are and where they need to go

Leaders must understand themselves, including their biases and assumptions, and have a great understanding of human psychology to lead and motivate people.

When we talk about the development of Self, we are looking at the individual. It is impossible to separate work life from other life, so we must make the best of both. Empowering people to take responsibility for their actions and the results they achieve has been linked to the potential for improving organizations. The common theme is that people need to feel a sense of mission or purpose along with the drive to make their goals reality. I truly believe that if people have a passion for what they do, they feel energized and committed, which results in a good sense of Self. These people are better team workers and better functioning people.

The most significant contributions that leaders make are to the long-term development of people and organizations that adapt, prosper, and grow. The challenge is to understand people in order to be able to assist them to reach their potential. We face the challenge of rapid assimilation of knowledge as we move from a society dominated by bureaucratic organizations to a complex global economy. Leadership is a critical factor in preparing people and organizations to continuously learn, grow, and develop. People who continue to work on themselves—through behavior modifications and development of relationships and technical skills—are better-functioning people. They are more committed, take more initiative, and have a broader and deeper sense of responsibility for themselves, their families, their work, their community, and life itself. Learning is a lifelong process. When people learn, then organizations have the ability to continuously change, meet customer needs, and be competitive.

Here is an exercise to help create your personal vision in an organizational environment or in your home environment. A personal vision is a tool not only for setting goals for ourselves but also for Self development. By committing to expand your personal capacity, you will not only produce most desired results but also master the principles underlying the way you produce the results.

Sit down in a quiet place that is quiet and private with no distractions. Take a few deep breaths, relaxing as you exhale. Once you have relaxed, begin brainstorming ideas about your aims, writing them on paper, in a notebook, or on a personal computer. Once you run out of ideas, look at your list and give a rating of 1 to 3 for each item on your list (1 is most important to you; 3 is least important). You will more than likely see a theme emerge from the 1s. Focus on this theme and determine what it is that you want to learn or know.

Next, you will create a result. This is Step 1. Bring yourself to a reflective frame of mind by taking a few deep breaths. Let go of any tension as you exhale so that you are relaxed, comfortable, and centered. Once relaxed, recall an image or memory that is meaningful to you; this could be a person, place, or event. Shut your eyes for a moment and try to stay with that image. Open your eyes and answer these questions: Imagine achieving a result in your life that you deeply desire. Ignore how possible or impossible this vision appears. Imagine your Self accepting the full manifestations of this result. Describe in writing (or sketch) the experience using present tense as if it's happening now. What does it look like? How does it feel? What words would you use to describe it?

Step 2 is reflecting on the vision. Did you articulate a vision that is close to what you actually want? Or did you find it hard to do because all these messages kept cluttering you mind—"I can't have what I want," "I want what someone else wants," "It doesn't matter what I want," "I already know what I want," "I'm afraid of what I want," "I don't know what I want," or "I know what I want, but I can't have it."

Step 3 is describing your personal vision. Imagine achieving the results in your life that you deeply desire. Describe each in how they would look and feel.

Self image: If you could be exactly the kind of person you wanted, what would your qualities be?

Tangibles: What material things would you like to own?

Home: What is your ideal living environment?

Health: What is your desire for health, fitness, and athletics?

Relationships: What types of relationships would you like to have with friends, family, and others?

Work: What is your ideal professional or vocational situation? What impact would you like your efforts to have?

Personal Pursuits: What would you like to create in the arena of individual learning, travel, reading, or other activities?

Community: What is your vision for the community or society you live in?

Other: What else, in any other arena of your life, would you like to create?

Life Purpose: Imagine that your life has a unique purpose—fulfilled through what you do, interrelationships and the way you live. Describe that purpose, as another reflection of your aspirations.

Step 4 is expanding and clarifying your vision. Go back to your list of components and ask yourself for each component: "If I could have it now, would I take it?" If you answer "No" or "Yes, but," amend your desire to something that you can say "Yes" to. Next, assume you have it. What does it bring to you? For example, if you wanted a Mercedes car because it would bring you a sense of freedom—what would you do with this freedom? What else could produce this sense of freedom? Maybe a healthy figure or physique so that you could play tennis better or make love for hours. Next, what themes or three or four primary goals emerge? What does it bring? For example, earlier in life my goal was to boost my income so that I could buy a house, live closer to my family, and have a sense of home and connection. I continued education which led to a higher paying position in the industry that resulted in our ability to purchase a home that was close to our families. Focused energies keep both a personal vision and a clear picture of current reality before you.

My life experience of my Personal Vision was that I wanted to teach. I brainstormed why I wanted to teach and what I would teach. My vision of what I hoped to gain was to teach others my knowledge and give students the skills to manage more effectively and efficiently after taking my class. My mission was to enhance the workplace and work environment so that people would feel more balanced in their lives and feel valued. The strategy I used was Peter Senge's concepts of the learning organization that focused on:

- systems thinking (closing silos and using open dialogue and communication)

- personal mastery (knowing yourself)

- mental models (understanding our biases, assumptions, and filters)

- team learning (understanding how we learn from each other)

- shared vision (integrating our personal vision and the organization's shared vision)

I also used the McKinsey Model 7S to analyze the strengths, weaknesses, opportunities, and threats in enhancing organizational effectiveness of:

- systems (evaluating procedures, information systems, performance measures, rewards, budget, controls)

- strategies (understanding how your business rates against competition)

- structure (identifying specialization and integration)

- skills (defining the competencies of the personnel)

- staffing (identifying the resources for the work needs)

- style (identifying what is done, not what is said)

- shared values (understanding the level of trust, integrity, morale, motivation and culture)

I also used the motivational grid, history of management theory and Myers-Briggs Type Indicator to provide a personality inventory based on the theories of Carl Jung. My objectives and goals were to teach using three methods—visual (show you), hearing (tell you), and doing (let you experience and experiment).

If you are a leader, you can take your personal vision one step further by creating a shared vision for your organization. Simply say, "What do we want to create?" There are many people involved in organizations, and each person has his/her own personal vision. The key is to create a shared vision for the organization that reflects each person's vision. In this way, you get commitment because the shared vision reflects individuals' own personal visions, thereby creating a sense of purpose, vision, and operating values that foster risk taking and experimentation.

Personal visions and shared visions are almost always simultaneous pursuits in organizations because people inevitably consider what they want for themselves. Shared vision is important for organizations to get people to participate and create where they want to be. It is part of creating meaningful work and part of creating buy-in so that they can do meaningful work.

For organizations, a shared vision is important to managing organizations. **You only get commitment from the employees when their personal vision and shared vision are aligned**.

It is my opinion that leaders must be taught the basic leadership skills. In addition to the ability to create a personal vision, another key skill is communications, the ability to listen and understand, especially what is not said. Effective communication is the ability to be in the here and now. For example, an effective communication tool is the Myers-Briggs Type Indicator, which is a process for self-evaluation and evaluation of how people think, how they approach things in life, and how they communicate. The MBTI provides people with insight for understanding how each of us is unique and different. We do not all perceive the world in the same way.

Another key skill is getting to know Self by learning and understanding your beliefs, assumptions, and filters. For example, I grew up in a family that was traditional. Boys played with trains, competed in sports, mowed lawns, and took out the garbage. Girls played with dolls and helped with the housework, dinner, and dishes. My father was a plumber; my mother was a nurse. I grew up thinking that I was never as good as men, that all I could be was a good wife and mother. It took a lot of years and a lot of work on me to get over that. Fortunately, boys and girls have equal opportunities in today's society. This is a good example of mental models.

We need to challenge our beliefs, assumptions, and filters. When we have an emotional reaction, we are having an assumption or bias against what is. An emotional reaction is when you feel your heart race, face flush, hair on the back of your neck stand up, tightness across your chest, sick feeling in the pit of your stomach, frustration or anger at what's being said. When you feel this emotional reaction, it is a good time to say, "Hmm, what does that mean?" It does not mean that you have an assumption that you should or should not have; it is just recognizing it. It may be an assumption that you don't want to give up. For example, I believe that violence is bad for people, and I have anger when I am witnessing violence. I probably won't give up my assumption that violence is bad. I want to hold onto it.

We need to learn to think and to understand how we think. How did you come to learn about thinking? What do you do? Where do you go? We each have role models, mentors, or others we emulate. Who do you emulate?

We learn about processing when we are young. For example, I have eight grandchildren. As a baby, each one learned that when he/she smiled, everyone smiled back and gives attention. Or, if a baby cried a lot, someone picked up the baby...so, the baby cries even more to be picked up. We each have different belief systems that get us to where we are.

My personal belief is that some of what we are, we are born with, and some of who we are, we learn at a very, very young age. We learn at home and from schools and environment.

If you are not thinking about what you are doing, you may do things out of behaviors learned. One way to challenge your assumptions and beliefs is to think about what you expect of guests when they come to your house. For example, if I were a guest at your house, what rules would I have to know to be a good guest? (i.e., no jumping on the furniture, eat what's served, no sleeping in the master bedroom, put the toilet seat back down after use). In another example, as I was watching my mother cook, she cut off the end of the roast before cooking. When I married, I cut off the end of the roast before cooking. Someone asked me why I cut off the end of the roast and threw it out. I didn't know. I asked my mother, who said she did it because her mother did. We found out that Granny did it because her roasting pan would not hold the whole roast. Ovens were smaller then, which doesn't apply to today's ovens.

Look at the things you do. Think about how you think. How do you know what you know? Those things that give you "recognizable" physical stress tell you about your assumptions. Those physical stress symptoms could be elevated heart rate, pain and tightness across the chest area, back ache, head ache, stomach ache. Be willing to challenge what you know.

Another key skill is conflict management, or the ability to diffuse a negative reaction into an open dialogue. Equally important is the key skill of interpersonal growth. This is the ability to reflect or sit quietly to understand yourself—who you are, what your purpose is, where you just came from, and where you are going. When asking yourself these questions, listen for the answers and follow them, especially if they feel right. If they don't feel right, change the direction you are going until it feels right.

Leaders must train and grow not only in an individual setting but also in a team environment that fosters and encourages trust. A team environment with developmental experiences allows people to learn and practice together and get better results. People who learn independently have a harder time integrating their learning into their work environment because there is no reinforcement for what people do. Leaders learn their most valuable lessons from others. For example, the 360-degree feedback tool solicits feedback from the management, peers, subordinates, and customers to identify the gap between where an individual should be and where the individual actually is in leadership and interpersonal skills.

All human beings want to be better than they are. People are eager to improve themselves. Self-improvement has an economic basis; however, our real growth is inward. We understand our spiritual selves through peace, silence, and beauty and in meditation and reflection. If we nourish the spirit, we can grow to be our better selves.

I believe that those leaders who have embraced both external and internal learning can sustain and maintain their level of Self by acting as mentors and coaches to facilitate others' growth. We are part of the whole…each one of us is part of the system that could include the universe, or it could be just a small group in an organization. **There is nothing more powerful you can do than to encourage others toward the lifelong process of working on Self.**

Chapter 7: A Self Development Exercise

A large part of development of Self is keeping your skills current, especially when technology is changing so rapidly that skill sets become obsolete quickly. The new economy requires new skills of computer literacy for the knowledge-based individual and the ability to work effectively in teams.

You must think of yourself as a business by defining your product and service, focusing on your area of expertise and your passion. Determine your target market by understanding why your employer would hire you or what your customer would buy from you. Once you are in a position of your choice, drive for quality work and satisfaction in everything that you do. Understand and know your field and how your skills fit in.

Most importantly, determine where is the field going and what skills might you need in the future. What does success look like? Invest in your own growth and development, including new products you will be able to provide. Be willing to change your business or job, or even start a new one.

The three foundation skills necessary in the workplace are basic, thinking, and personal qualities. Basic skills include reading, writing, mathematics, speaking, and listening. Thinking skills include creativity, decision making, problem solving, knowing how to learn, and reasoning. Personal qualities include responsibility, self-esteem, sociability, self-management, and integrity.

The five job skills needed in the workplace are resources, interpersonal, information, systems, and technology. Resources include allocating time, money, materials, space, and staff. Interpersonal includes effectively working on teams, teaching, serving customers, leading and mentoring others, negotiating, and working well with people from culturally diverse backgrounds. Information includes acquiring and evaluating data, organizing and maintaining files, interpreting and communicating, and using computers to process information. Systems include understanding social, organizational, and technological systems; monitoring and correcting performance; and designing improved systems. Technology includes selecting equipment and tools necessary to do a successful job, applying technology to specific tasks, and maintaining and trouble-shooting technologies.

Those individuals with effective interpersonal communication skills are better able to cope with change. The ability to change direction quickly determines how quickly an organization rebounds or is revitalized when change occurs. This can also be applied to all areas of an individual's life.

A twenty-five-year-old engineering graduate will have to be reeducated eight times within a forty-year career to keep skills current, especially when technology is changing so rapidly that skill sets become obsolete quickly. When we talk about effective interpersonal communication skills, we are really talking about relationships. **One of the key stumbling blocks to effective communications is dealing with conflict, which is why it is important to know about your Self.** When we talk about dialogue and relationships, we have conflict, which is normal. The way we deal with conflict is the key to effective relationships.

I like to talk about a couple of television shows: *Leave It to Beaver* with Hugh Beaumont (Ward Cleaver), and *I Love Lucy* with Lucille Ball (Lucy Ricardo), Desi Arnaz (Ricky Ricardo), Vivian Vance (Ethel Mertz), and William Frawley (Fred Mertz). Everyone is either high, low, or in between on relationships and high, low, or in between on control. Here is a chart that helps you understand the styles of dealing with conflict for each person in this series.

Look at each person on the chart—Ethel, Lucy, Ward, Fred, and Ricky.

Styles of Dealing with Conflict

	High				
		Ethel		Lucy	
Concern for Relationship		Ward			
		Fred		Ricky	
	Low			High	
		Concern for Control			

Ethel is high on concern for relationship and low on concern for control. Lucy is high on concern for relationship and high on concern for control. Ward is in the middle on concern for relationship and for concern for control. Fred is low on concern for relationship and low on concern for control. Ricky is low on concern for relationship and high on concern for control. What does this mean when someone is dealing with conflict?

- Ricky Style: likes to win; leader; self-directed; motivated, in charge; win-oriented (my way only); get the job done. This style may hurt relationships because this person always wants his way. Others may feel hurt and resentful if their thoughts are not considered. Encourage reaching out and considering others thoughts and feelings.

- Lucy Style: affirmation, encouragement, and applause; a party waiting to happen; talks a lot; networks; knows everyone. This type of person is hard to trust sometimes because you don't know if he or she is repeating to others your confidences. Encourage them to keep confidences.

- Ethel Style: most people fall into this category; loves relational people; knows how to communicate; listens; shows empathy; builds trust; loyal. These people do not deal with conflict; they submit needs to others, repress or deny feelings and internalize and pull away (isolate or get sick). These are "do not rock the boat" type of people. Encourage them to feel safe and take risks.

- Fred Style: avoidance; does not deal with conflict. This type of person is low on concern for relationships and low on concern for control. Encourage them to get involved.

- Ward Style: the balanced person; talks and listens; closes the loop to resolve conflict; goes beyond compromise; maintains relationships.

The *San Francisco Chronicle* ran an article in the aftermath of the 2000 presidential election that referred to *I Love Lucy's* "The Club Election" episode. In that episode, Lucy and Ethel tied in a race for club president. What do you think happened, given that both Lucy and Ethel were "feeling" types where relationship and harmony were most important? They decided to become copresidents and share the power. The article said that Al Gore and George W. Bush should follow their lead and become coleaders of the free world. If Gore and Bush had had the sense—not to mention the charisma—of wacky Lucy, they would not have been in such a mess.

Once you understand how you, your friends, family, and coworkers deal with conflict, you will be able to better build trust and manage your relationships and work effectively in teams.

Chapter 8: Effective Teams

A large part of managing organizations and relationships is forming effective teams. Teams and groups come together when they develop a shared vision, mission, goals, and objectives. The advantages of forming teams are better work processes and outcomes, better decisions, and the awareness of the most important issues so that you can reach consensus. The key elements in forming effective teams or groups include understanding yourself, understanding others, communicating effectively, and building relationships.

One of the elements includes understanding yourself and others. The Myers-Briggs Type Indicator (MBTI) personality preference instrument is one of the most widely used tools in businesses around the world and has been in existence for more than sixty years.

The sixteen Myers-Briggs types are based on Jungian theory that we all have natural, inborn preferences for doing certain things. To illustrate our preferences, try this exercise.

- Take out a piece of paper and write your full name.

    o   Once you have written your name, notice that it feels very natural.

- Now, write your name again with your opposite hand.

    o   Notice that it feels awkward and unnatural.

You could use your unnatural preference when forced; however, we are all born with a natural preference for the way we do things.

The MBTI preferences fall into four categories: Extraversion/Introversion (where we get our energy), Sensing/Intuition (how we gather information), Thinking/ Feeling (how we make decisions and solve problems), and Judging/Perceiving (what our orientation is).

Extraverts tend to focus on the outer world of people and external events and get their energy from others. Introverts tend to focus on their own inner world of ideas and experiences and get their energy from within.

Here's a story about an Extravert (Mary Ellen) and an Introvert (Tom). They were driving home one evening and the trip took about two hours. It was a nice leisurely pace. Tom dropped Mary Ellen off at her house and said, "I'll talk to you tomorrow." Mary Ellen turned to Tom and said, "Aren't we going to spend any time together?" Tom said, "Well, we just did."

To Tom, the quiet time together was quality time together; Mary Ellen was looking for more activity and interaction (external). She assumed that he did not want to be with her. In reality, he needed time alone to reenergize.

Sensing people prefer to take in information through their eyes, ears, and other senses. Intuitive people prefer to take information in by seeing the big picture, focusing on the relationship and connections between facts.

A quick and clear way to think about Sensing and Intuitive people is to ask a question, "Where is the restroom"? When an Intuitive gives directions to a Sensing, he/she cannot imagine how the directions could have been more clearly defined, but the person gets lost. The Intuitive gives more imaginative or creative direction. A Sensing person would give specific detail, street by street and turn by turn, including landmarks.

Thinking people tend to make decisions by looking at the logical sequences of a choice or action. They try to mentally remove themselves from a situation to examine it objectively and analyze the cause and effect. Feeling people tend to consider what is important to them and to other people. They mentally place themselves in a situation and identify with the people involved so that they can make decisions based on person-centered values.

How does this translate to the workplace? Let's say Jeff, the boss, wants some project update information from Steve. Jeff is a Sensing type and he wants detailed information. If Steve just gives him the big picture, it will drive Jeff crazy. He will demand more information before he makes a decision. The opposite is true as well. If Mary is an Intuitive type, she would only want the "big picture." Too many details would put an Intuitive into tilt mode.

Here is an exercise that you can use in determining Sensing or Intuitive types. In a room, place two groups of chairs in a circle. At the center of each group of chairs and approximately three feet from the chairs, place a plain coffee mug. Ask the folks who think they are Sensing to sit in one group and the people who think they are Intuitive to sit in the other group. Their task is to describe what they see in the center. The Sensing people will want to touch it and feel it. They will describe in detail that it is blue with a handle and hold six ounces of coffee. The Intuitives will see the mug, but they will describe someone sitting on a patio sipping coffee in the morning sun.

You can see where you have a challenge in communication when one person has a preference for detail and how it was done in the past whereas another person wants to look at all the possibilities of how it could be done differently.

Here is another exercise that might be helpful. Management has asked you to determine the criteria to be used when deciding who is to be laid off.

Here are the facts:

- Two out of eight people on a work team must be laid off.

Everyone in the team:

- has been with the organization for the same length of time

- does essentially the same kind of work

- has been evaluated as having approximately the same level of performance

When students were asked to come up with some ideas, here is what they suggested:

- present the situation to the team;

- ask the members for ideas on how to handle the situation (i.e., shorter work week for each person to keep all eight);

- ask if there are any volunteers who would like to be laid off; and,

- if there are no volunteers, select two people with the most challenging fit to the team based on the MBTI.

When managing organizations and problem solving, the Intuitive misses out on the details while the Sensing misses out on other possibilities. It's extremely important to have both types on a team, working together and listening to bring balance to the outcome of the project.

Judging people process in the outer world and tend to live in a planned, orderly way, wanting to regulate and control life. They make decisions, come to closure, and move on. Perceiving people process in the outer world and tend to live in a flexible, spontaneous way, seeking to experience and understand life, rather than control it. Plans and decisions feel confining to them; they prefer to stay open to experience any last-minute options.

If you have a preference for Judging, you want things planned and structured and have a need for closure. You make lists and live by them. Judging people are like a rudder on a ship. Set the direction, and you can count on these people to keep heading in that direction. The beauty is that you can count on them to get you there. The downside is…remember the *Titanic*? With new information, Judging types ignore and continue on the same path or direction. Perceiving types, however, are at the bow of the ship saying, "Let's go this way; let's go that way. I wonder what's over there." Perceiving types are more spontaneous and want to keep options open.

Here's a story. A little kid is looking out the window of his house at floodwaters rushing down the street. He sees debris floating. He sees a baseball cap at the edge of the water going back and forth in front of his house. He calls to his mother, "Come and look at this hat going back and forth in front of our house when everything else is going down toward Tommy's house!" His mother says, "Oh, don't worry about that, that's your father. He said he was going to mow the lawn come hell or high water."

As you can see, Judging types prefer to stick to their schedule and commitments and use lists. Perceiving types lose lists because they want to be spontaneous.

How does the difference between Judging and Perceiving play out in the work world? When schedules change, it's an issue for Judging. Judging gets things organized and moves in direction toward results. Perceiving plays the devil's advocate and asks or sees the possibilities.

The MBTI provides a straightforward and affirmative path to self-understanding as well as understanding of others. It offers a logical model of consistent human behavior, including emphasizing the value of diversity and uniqueness, especially when forming teams and groups.

When becoming a part of a team, it's important that you understand your preferences as well as the preferences of others. John became part of a leadership team that consisted of a manager, three supervisors, and a technical consultant. With MBTI training, he was able to observe the group at many levels and understand the team dynamics. The group met weekly to communicate information, determine future needs, and resolve problems that might have hindered the department's success.

Samantha, the managing director was a thirty-five-year-old middle-class Caucasian. She was raised in a small Midwestern town and had an engineering degree. She was an Extravert, Intuitive, Feeling, and Judging personality type. The behaviors she exhibited included talking frequently, initiating discussions, and responding emotionally to the team members. She had high energy, initiated information and opinion seeking, provided gatekeeping, and expressed group feelings. She was people-oriented and responsive to the needs of the people she supervised. Samantha was well matched for her leadership roles in the organization and on the team.

Brian was one of the supervisors. He was an Introvert, Sensing, Thinking, Judging personality type. He was a forty-eight-year-old middle-class Asian raised in the Bay Area and had an engineering degree. The behaviors he exhibited included a traditional, hierarchical approach and a desire to get things done. His role in the group was to focus on the tasks or activities that needed to be done. He was an initiator and was extremely structured.

Another supervisor, Gary was an Extravert, Sensing, Feeling, Perceiving personality type. This fifty-two-year-old middle-class Caucasian was raised in the Bay Area and had an engineering degree. The behaviors he exhibited included presenting a positive image of the organization to others, offering actions and excitement, and accepting and dealing with people as they were. He brought harmony to the group and was energetic and easygoing. His role in the group was that of focusing on the tasks and maintaining the relationships.

The third supervisor, Rich, was an Extravert, Intuitive, Feeling, and Perceiving personality type. The thirty-eight-year-old middle-class Hispanic was raised in a small town in the Southwest and had an engineering degree. The behaviors he exhibited included high energy and enthusiasm, originating projects and actions, encouraging and showing appreciation of others. He was unconstrained and idea oriented. His role in the group was focusing on the tasks or activities, as well as providing a vision of the anticipated outcome or result wanted.

Isabel was the technical consultant. She was an Extravert, Sensing, Thinking, Judging personality type. She was a forty-four-year-old middle-class Caucasian, raised in the East, with a bachelor's degree in business administration and finance. The behaviors she exhibited included respecting hierarchy and adapting well to solving problems. Her role in the group was focusing on the tasks. She gave information and provided clarification of any confusing information frequently.

John, the newest member of the group, was an Introvert, Intuitive, Feeling, Judging personality type. The fifty-five-year-old middle-class Caucasian was raised in the Bay Area. John had an MBA as well as a master's in organizational psychology. The behaviors he exhibited included lending stability to the organization, using personal influence behind the scenes, helping those who needed support, and offering a calm, quiet, conscientious presence.

When this team first met with John in attendance, he noticed struggles with identity, control and influence, personal needs, and acceptance. Working norms had not been established at this point, as was evidenced by a fair amount of tension in the group. Isabel was matter-of-fact and not interested in subjects she saw no use for which did not take into account Gary's need for common sense and practical ability. John observed some aggressive coping, support-seeking coping and withdrawal behaviors. Aggressive coping can be rejecting others' suggestions or interrupting. Support-seeking coping is sharing issues and turning to others for support or affiliation. Withdrawal behaviors are detaching from the group or a lack of interest in finding common areas of agreement.

One observable behavior was interrupting. Rich interrupted Isabel. John waited until Rich was through and then asked Isabel if that was what she was trying to say. She said no and began to explain. Later, Rich interrupted when Samantha was talking. John waited until Rich was through and then asked Samantha if that was what she was trying to say. She also said no and began to clarify. By the third time, Rich began listening until the other person finished.

When John first brought the behavior into the open, he could see by Rich's body language that he felt uncomfortable. Once Rich modified his behavior, the team members began to be more open and responsive. Rich's need for power and control, exhibited by interrupting, inhibited the working of the group. When he stopped interrupting, members felt heard. It's important that each member feels heard; this gives the person a sense of belonging by providing meaningful information. **When people feel they are important to the group, they begin to work together in a trusting relationship.**

Another observable behavior was the use of, "Yes, but…" by Brian. John thought about how to tackle this behavior and decided to do it offline. Even though it would have been better to have approached the behavior in the group and used "I" statements to express frustration and hurt feelings, John wanted to handle this behavior on a one-on-one with Brian so he would not embarrass him in front of the group. Outside of the group, John asked Brian about the issue. After Brian finished what he was saying, John immediately said, "Yes, but…" and told him his thoughts. John noticed Brian's body language and asked him what his reaction was to him at that moment. Brian said he was "pissed." John told him that he understood. They then discussed the use of "Yes, but…" and how folks react to it because it negates what is said before the word *but*, leaving the person frustrated and angry.

John then checked in with Brian, who confirmed that this was how he felt when John used that phrase. They then talked about words to use to get thoughts heard without invalidating the other person's ideas. John suggested that Brian acknowledge the person's idea by saying, "That's a good point. Have you considered…" In this way, you are honoring the other person's opinion and are able to get the other person to think about additional information in a non-threatening way.

John sensed that Brian's use of the "Yes, but…" was his way of attempting to control and structure according to his personal needs for organization and task. The behavior change contributed in a positive way to the effective functioning of the leadership team.

Another observable behavior that John influenced was the use of harmonizing and compromising. With the group focusing on task, relationships appeared to suffer. Finding common areas of interest and needs such as asking what part was absolutely needed in their area and what they could do without being helped reestablish good communication and connected personal needs for the good of the group.

After two months, John compared the similarities and differences in his group's effectiveness, including communicating and group problem-solving skills. His conclusions:

The team has a good mixture of folks
for problem solving and working effectively

in light of ambiguity in the future. Brian and Gary (Sensing) want to know the facts, details, and all views; Isabel (Thinking) wants to know the pros and cons, logical sequence, and consequences; Rich (Intuitive) wants to know the implications beyond the facts; and Samantha (Feeling) wants harmony, reacts to all emotionally, and brings values.

Let Samantha, Gary, Rich, and Isabel, the Extraverts, talk and include a variety of topics. Communicate orally. Ask them to listen. Brian and John are the Introverts. They need to ask others to listen because they only like one person talking at a time. They need time to reflect and prepare.

Samantha, Rich, and John are Intuitives and talk about the big picture and possibilities. Use analogies and metaphors. Encourage their imagination. They do not like to be overwhelmed with details. Isabel, Brian, and Gary want the topic stated clearly with facts and examples. Sensing folks stress practical application and present information step-by-step.

Samantha, Gary, and John are Feeling. They want points of agreement mentioned. They appreciate the efforts and contributions of others. They recognize the legitimacy of feelings and enjoy dealing with people. They are concerned with relationships. Brian and Isabel are Thinking and want things organized and logical. They appeal to the sense of fairness. They are concerned with tasks, not relationships.

Samantha, Brian, Isabel, and John are Judging types. They want people to be on time and prepared. They want folks to be decisive and definitive. They want things resolved. Do not waste their time. Gary and Rich are Perceiving types. They have many questions and do not want decisions forced on them, so allow time and an opportunity to discuss options. These folks want choices.

After the group began functioning as a team, group interests rather than personal needs had become the main concern. The group was more open and responsive. The members had gained confidence from becoming more familiar with each other as well as responding favorably to some of John's interventions. John helped change behaviors with interventions that included paraphrasing others, soliciting feedback on issues when body language suggested that members were either tuned out or not in agreement, and by demonstrating honesty and integrity in his working with the group.

The connection between the subtle communication processes and the factual exchange is required for effective working relations. This has been an example of a group that has dealt with the basics of communication and has been able to work effectively as a group in the problem-solving and decision-making roles.

Understanding your preferences and others preferences is the first step in forming teams. Once a team is formed, there are stages of development or group development that are important to effective team functioning.

Chapter 9: Team Development and Stages of Group Development

We just talked about understanding your and others' preferences as the first steps in forming teams. Two additional factors are important to effective team functioning: group development and effective interpersonal relationships.

There are four stages of development for a group:

- Stage One, dependency and inclusion; some of you might call it forming

- Stage Two, counterdependency and fight or "storming"

- Stage Three, trust and structure; when group members come to consensus, sometimes called "norming"

- Stage Four, work; the group is performing

In Stage One, team members are dependent and want to feel included. They will make mental notes of their first impressions of others. For example, Sam comes into a room and spreads papers all around a lot of space. Some people may see him as controlling and desiring a lot of space. Others may see him as a hard worker who really has it together; he has everything he needs. Depending on who you are, you are going to have different views or thoughts about each person.

As the group begins to know one another, Sam discloses that he spent two years in jail for robbing a bank. Immediately, your impression of him changes. You look at him and say, "He doesn't look like a criminal." Then, you think, but he did spend two years in prison. Your next thought is, "He's not like me because my values are that I do not rob banks." Then you find out that Sam was a teller in a bank and that he was framed by somebody who was caught after two years. Your impression changes again.

When forming a team, it is important to really look at what you see in other people. People who become members of a team are concerned with issues such as: personal safety; acceptance and inclusion; am I going to fit in; are you going to like me; are you going to treat me as an equal; and, am I going to be able to contribute with what I know. Our mind is continuously trying to determine if we are dominant or submissive or top or bottom so that we know how to play the role. Members of a new group fear rejection. Keep this in mind when you are in a new work group or team-based project. Everyone in the group experiences some or all of these elements.

In Stage One, members communicate in a polite manner and never get past being polite. Subgroups and coalitions are rare at this stage. Overt conflict is minimal. There may be some individuals who are vocal, but usually only a few. If you are a facilitator or the informal group leader, your main purpose is to get the group beyond this stage or the group will never perform.

During the first stage, roles and assignments are based on external status and first impressions rather than matching competencies with goals. During this stage, member compliance is high. Communication such as groupthink is centralized. Participation is limited to a few vocal members. The group lacks group structure. Member deviation from group norms is rare during this stage. Cohesion with the group is based on identification with the leader. Once the group begins to feel comfortable, it will move to Stage Two.

In Stage Two, the team members will begin to reveal their personal goals, assumptions, and expectations. This is the stage where you as the leader or facilitator state expectations and what will be measured. Members will express concerns with original group goals. Some will even challenge the leader. Subgroups and coalitions may form. At this point, conflicts will surface, and disagreements about goals and tasks will emerge. Conflict resolution, if successful, increases consensus about group goals and culture near the end of this stage. Conflict resolution also increases trust and cohesion and results in increased member participation.

During this stage, you begin to reveal some of their assumptions whether or not you are aware of it. You start to reveal something about yourself and learn that others see the world differently. Conflicts about values begin to surface. Have you ever been to a meeting where the steps you had to take to get to the end result were so clear? Then, all of a sudden, someone else came at it from another point of view (like Mars). You either thought to yourself or said, "Hello. That's not going to work." If you stay in this mode, it's debilitating. You must be able to recognize when this happens and move on to the next stages because that's where a lot of creativity begins.

Forming subgroups is detrimental to the group's progress. Let's say you have ten members working on a task and two members go off and talk on their own. They return saying, "We think…" The leader or facilitator needs to say, "Wait a minute. It's not us against you; we want as a team to get you here." You do not want alliances to form that interfere with the group's progress. You want to move through this stage as fast as you can.

In Stage Three, trust and structure are evident due to increased goal clarity and consensus of what the group wants. The leader's role becomes less directive and more consultative. For example, a group of fourteen team members were asked, "Do you want A or B?" The three members who were the most vocal said, B, and no one else spoke. The group waited for the leader to say B. After a few minutes of silence, the leader asked, "What about the rest of you?" He then waited as some folks started to fidget in their seats. The leader was inviting other opinions without saying that he'd like to hear from the others. One of the members finally said she wanted A. When that person spoke up, seven others said they would prefer A. If the leader had gone with the verbal people, he would not have had consensus on what the members really wanted. Not all of the team members are going to be vocal about their wants and desires. It's up to the leader or informal leader to ask these members what their thoughts are to encourage participation.

In Stage Four, the work progresses because the members are clear about and agree with the goals. Members are also clear about their roles and assignments that match their abilities. This is the stage when the work gets done and results are measured and rewarded. The best performance is when the group is in sync. You can witness this level of performance in team sports. Some teams are out there playing the game with very little effort, whereas other teams are playing at high level and with great passion. Some might even say that the team experiences a group phenomenon at this level. It's called "the zone" in team sports, but it can be the experience of any good, functioning team.

Every team's success depends on effective interpersonal communication because as with all teams you will experience conflict. Effective interpersonal communication helps people cope with change and determines how quickly an organization rebounds or is revitalized when change occurs. Sometimes an employee detaches emotionally from the change or refuses to acknowledge the traditional role of the supervisor. To engage the employee, the supervisor must be open, supportive, and empowering.

Conflict occurs in situations in which people are interdependent, seek different outcomes, favor different methods to the same end, or perceive others are interfering with their ability for rewards or resources. A person's behavior in conflict situations can be described by two basic dimensions—assertiveness and cooperation. Assertiveness is the extent to which the team member attempts to satisfy his own concerns. Cooperation is the team members attempt to satisfy the other person's concerns. There are five specific methods of dealing with conflict using these two dimensions: competing, collaborating, compromising, avoiding, and accommodating. Each one of us has a tendency for one or more behavior styles depending on the situation.

Conflict Behavior Styles

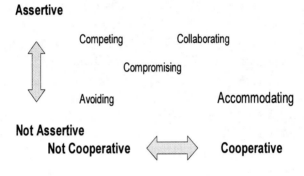

Competing behavior is assertive, not cooperative. It reflects the desire to meet your own needs and concerns at the expense of the other person. These people use whatever power they have available such as position, information, persuasive ability, or coercion. This style may be damaging to a team because the person is on his/her own agenda and not likely to want to hear about what others want. This style may be appropriate in a life-threatening situation when there is a dangerous circumstance that may need immediate control without considering the needs of others.

Collaborating behavior is both cooperative and assertive with the desired result satisfying the needs and concerns of both people. This style requires tremendous commitment and takes considerable time and energy. Collaborating is used when the concerns of the people are extremely important and cannot be ignored. It involves examining values, assumptions, and possible solutions. We find that creative ideas and solutions to complex problems have a greater possibility to emerge through collaborating.

Avoiding behavior is considered not cooperative and not assertive. People who use this style avoid the conflict and are indifferent to each other's needs and concerns. This type of style can be used effectively as either an interim or a permanent strategy. For example, in a heated discussion, it may be beneficial to allow the other person to cool down. Another example would be when you need more information or more time to make a decision. Too much avoidance can create problems; when the decision is made and goals are set without others' input, the result is poor implementation and low levels of commitment. However, selective avoidance is a good way to keep from becoming overwhelmed by conflict.

Accommodating behavior is characterized by cooperative and not assertive. These people are generally quiet. They are people who put others' needs and concerns above their own, even if they have strong needs and concerns themselves. Accommodating does build goodwill and leads to cooperative relationships. It preserves harmony and avoids disruption when one person has more power than the other. The downside is that those who use accommodating to excess may feel that their own ideas, needs, and concerns are not receiving the attention they deserve and may erode their influence, respect, and recognition from others. Long-term effects of accommodating behavior can be internalized anger and invalidation.

Compromising behavior is halfway between competing and collaborating and avoiding and accommodating. The person compromising anticipates a partial fulfillment of needs, concerns, and goals in the outcome. Although the solution reached through compromising is mutually acceptable, it only partially satisfies each person's needs and desires. Compromise is appropriate and effective for temporary solutions, including when the goals of the people involved are moderately important. People who always compromise sometimes lose sight of important values and other possibilities. Conversely, those who never compromise may never develop the skills needed to bargain or negotiate.

When teams form, there will be conflict. When two people are together, there will be conflict. Any time there is more than one person, you will have conflict. How do you handle conflict?

Here's an exercise to help recognize how you deal with conflict.

Of the following statements on the next page, please choose and circle either "A" or "B" for the statement that best characterizes your behavior when your desires or wants differ from another.

1A. Sometimes I let others take responsibility for solving problems.
1B. Rather than negotiate our differences, I stress areas that we agree upon.

2A. I try to find a compromise solution.
2B. I attempt to deal with all of the other's concerns as well as my own.

3A. I am usually firm in attaining my goals.
3B. I try to soothe the other persons feelings to maintain our relationship.

4A. I try to postpone the issue until I have had more time to think about it.
4B. I give up some of my wants in exchange for the other person's wants.

5A. I propose a middle of the ground solution.
5B. I stand firm to get my points made.

6A. I express my ideas and ask for others' ideas.
6B. I attempt to demonstrate the logic and benefits of my position.

7A. I try to get all concerns and issues out in the open.
7B. I try to postpone the issue until I have had time to think it over.

8A. If the other person has an important position, I try to meet his wishes.
8B. I try to get the other person to agree to a compromise.

Now turn this page and score your answers. The results will give you an understanding of your preference style when dealing with conflict.

Scoring

Using the chart below, circle the Answer you chose from previous page.

#	Compete	Collaborate	Compromise	Avoid	Accommodate
1				1A	1B
2		2B	2A		
3	3A				3B
4			4B	4A	
5	5B		5A		
6	6B	6A			
7		7A		7B	
8			8B		8A

Enter below the Total the number of items circled in each column above.

Compete	Collaborate	Compromise	Avoid	Accommodate

The column with the highest score characterizes your behavior when your desires or wants differ from another.

Understanding the style with which you are comfortable is important when you are dealing with conflict with one person or in a group. For example, if avoidance is how you deal with conflict, when it arises, you will shrink back, saying to yourself, "I don't want to do this." Your thoughts might go like, "It's bad enough when it happens with my spouse, but I don't have to do it in my job."

Keep in mind that there are times when every one of these behaviors will appear in each of us. For example, we would not have sports without competitive conflict—football, baseball, basketball, hockey, golf. People get a charge out of this type of competition. There is excitement about who is going to win or lose. There is value in accommodating and compromising. There is value in each behavior, depending on what you need for the given situation.

Conflict has value. If you discourage conflict, you will have trouble building good teams. If everyone always agrees, we go along and it's boring and predictable. But what if you don't want yelling, screaming and hitting? That kind of conflict scares me. It reminds me of my childhood. But, when we talk about conflict, we are really talking about our differences. Our differences are who we are. Knowing that each person is different allows us to go into a group or team with the understanding that everyone will have different opinions and thoughts. But if we think everyone is the same, we will be really disappointed and hurt when someone differs from us.

Here is a conflict exercise that I used when teaching students. I would say to a group, "Ice cream" and ask, "What do you see?" Some would say a flavor such as vanilla, strawberry, or chocolate. But someone may have thought that I said, "I scream" because they came from an abusive background. When they heard "I scream," they felt the emotion fear.

Here is another example of showing our differences. What if I said, "Let's talk about racism"? Often, there is an emotional charge because people come from a place of different experiences, beliefs, and assumptions. Instead, I might ask, "What's your experience with racism?" I will hear more by listening to your thoughts and beliefs. You can de-escalate conflict by asking questions on topics that you believe might be charged with emotion.

We each have the responsibility to be aware of the differences and uniqueness in each of us. Conflict is good. Be open to differences. Until each of us can say, "Tell me what you think; let me hear what you think; and, why do you believe what you think," then the conflict will continue to be competing. Using inquiry and questions to find out more about the other person will give us understanding and compassion.

These are some of the behaviors that get in the way of a good, functioning team:

- Deflating other people's ideas ("That's a stupid idea")

- Resisting by being negative ("That won't work")

- Pushing your own ideas without listening ("Only my idea will work")

- Seeking constant attention (too loud or too verbal)

- Being cynical ("Yeah, right!")

- Leaving the team psychologically/mentally (daydreaming)

These are some of the behaviors that help a team function effectively:

- Bringing issues or problems to the team's attention
- Asking for and giving information
- Assisting the group by clarifying ideas
- Summarizing to help with understanding what's been said
- Identifying areas that are common to all
- Trying to bring things to conclusions
- Attempting to reconcile and find common ground in a disagreement
- Encouraging participation
- Being friendly
- Setting standards, including being accountable and responsible
- Maintaining the momentum of the team
- Using humor

Sometimes, groups get stuck because they don't know where they are going and they don't know how to get there. They could be stuck on resources or conflict, or they could have strayed from the objectives and need redirection. To help them move forward, define the objectives and clarify priorities. In addition, assist the team in creating Action Plans that list major steps needed to get from what is now to where you want to be.

We have reviewed the stages of team and group development and effective interpersonal relationships and defined what behaviors help a team and discussed how to move a team forward that might be stuck. One of the most reliable indicators of a team that is continually learning is the visible conflict of ideas. **Teams that have a good understanding of conflict management work effectively and learn to trust others**. These people work together effectively in other subgroups, are more task oriented, demonstrate increased satisfaction, and work toward better decisions.

Chapter 10: History of Leadership—Four Main Eras

New paradigms result from the movement and societal changes from premodern era to the current information/knowledge age. These changes necessitate different characteristics for leaders managing organizations. We have all experienced these changes through generations in our own lives and in our own homes and families. The following chart summarizes the environment, currency, organization, and power source for each of the four main eras: premodern, modern, postmodern, and information/knowledge.

Leadership – Four Main Eras

	Environment	Currency	Organization	Power Source
Premodern (Pre-Industrial)	Agriculture or Manufacture	Property Owners	Church	Land/Physical
Modern (1850-1940)	Large Monopolies	Money	Corporation	Money/Social
Postmodern 1940 - 1980	Partnerships or Alliances	Knowledge or Information	Organizations	Intellectual
Information Age 1980 - Current	Coach/Mentor	Work/Life Balance	Community	Spiritual

During the pre-modern era, wise leaders led small, limited resources. These folks were good communicators. During the modern era, brave leaders led monopolies that were large and continued to expand resources, including establishing boundaries to protect resources. The focus was on control and management with communication top down. During the post-modern era, visionary leaders led large organizations with more flexible boundaries to maximize resources. They empowered the workforce. The focus was on leadership, not management. Communication was from the bottom up.

During the information/knowledge age, empowered, shared leadership has eliminated boundaries and created virtual organizations. Organizations are maximizing leadership by focusing on shared leadership and inter-dependence. There is excellent communication systemwide. The need for workers in the information disciplines is going up, and the need for blue-collar workers is going down. Recently, a longshoreman position was advertised. The pay was exceptional, considering that the job required physical work and no technical skills. Over three thousand people applied. We are creating fewer and fewer jobs for the blue collar working class who I believe will become poorer and poorer.

As we create a poorer and poorer class, I believe we will have more uprisings, more anger, more violence, more "You can't do this." Unless we are willing to educate whole groups of people into new jobs, then we won't really be moving forward in this new paradigm in business. **As a society, we need to address what we are doing to provide education to those who are unable to become formally educated**.

The characteristics of the new knowledge worker are good communication skills, college education, self-reliance, generalist, connected in team-based projects, specialist (expert), ability to apply analytical and theoretical learning, and commitment to lifelong learning.

It is very important that people continue to learn to help with the economical and societal paradigm shift into the information age.

Chapter 11: How to Motivate Others

Motivation is one of the key skills that leaders managing organizations want to develop. Motivation is the leader's ability to urge action in others by influencing their inner drive.

Motivation has always been a popular subject. How can we influence someone we cannot motivate? When I was a teacher, students always were attentive during this lecture. As a first-level supervisor, I used the methodology in this chapter to provide the right environment for the employees for maximum productivity and efficiency of operation. When increased level of responsibility moved me into a second-level supervisor position, I used the methodology on the first-level supervisors who reported to me. The first-level supervisors used the training to motivate their employees.

The key concept to motivation is that effective leadership is situational, meaning the leader adopts different leadership styles depending on the situation.

An instructor once said, "A leader is a follower is a leader." What this means is that the leadership style used is guided by the needs of the follower. Flexibility in leading and understanding your employee or the person you are trying to motivate is key. Even though the leadership style should be guided by the needs of the follower, leaders will commonly fall into a certain style.

There are several leadership and management styles as shown in the Managerial Grid.

MANAGERIAL GRID
Management/Leadership Styles

	HIGH				
		Country Club Management		Team Management	
Concern for People			Organization Management		
		Impoverished Management		Authority or Obedience Management	
	LOW				**HIGH**
			Concern for Production		

The left axis shows the leaders who have a concern for people. The scale goes from high to low. The bottom axis shows the leaders who have a concern for production.

The **country club management** style, in the top left corner, pays a great deal of attention to the needs of people and satisfying relationships. The atmosphere of this organization is friendly and comfortable.

The top right corner is **team management** style, is an environment in which committed people working as a team or in teams accomplish the work. These people share trust and respect as well as interdependence through a common stake.

The lower left corner is the **impoverished management** style, which indicates minimum effort to get the required work done. This type of leader only sustains or maintains the organization.

The lower right corner is **authority or obedience management** style, a very efficient operation with human elements involved only to a minimum degree. This type of leader is the taskmaster.

At the middle of the grid is the **organization management** style, indicating a balance between the getting the work done and maintaining a satisfactory level of morale.

Which is the best management style?

Over 1,500 companies were sampled using the hypothesis that the best managers should be team management—high on relations and tasks. However, the Fortune 100 companies were right in the **middle**—using an organization management with a balance between work and the employee needs.

Best Managers . . .

RELATIONS			
	High on Relations Low on Tasks	High on Relations High on Tasks	
	Low on Relations Low on Tasks	Low on Relations High on Tasks	
			TASKS

Once you know a leader's style of management in terms of the amount of direction and support, you can then look at four approaches used, based on relations and tasks. The approaches are supporting, guiding or coaching, delegating, and telling or directing.

LEADERSHIP APPROACHES

RELATIONS			
	Supporting	Guiding or Coaching	
	Delegating	Telling or Directing (Hands On)	
			TASKS

The **supporting** approach shares ideas and facilitates discussion and involvement. The **guiding or coaching** approach explains decisions and provides opportunity for clarification. The **delegating** leadership approach turns over responsibility for decision making and implementation. Finally, the **telling or directing** approach provides specific hands-on direction.

Once you have determined your leadership style and approach, you will go to the next step: determining the follower's readiness for the specific task. The follower is the employee. To be a successful leader, you must be able to analyze the readiness of the follower's maturity level as well as his or her professional level.

READINESS OF FOLLOWER

PROFESSIONAL MATURITY	**PSYCHOLOGICAL MATURITY**

▪ ABILITY OR CAPACITY
- KNOWLEDGE
- TRAINING
- EXPERIENCE

▪ MOTIVATION (WILLINGNESS TO DO)
- REWARDS
- RECOGNITION
- CONFIDENCE
- SELF ESTEEM

Professional maturity is the person's ability or capacity based on his or her knowledge, training, and experience. Psychological maturity is the person's motivation or willingness to do the task. You cannot measure these, but they are very much part of motivation. Psychological maturity includes

- rewards, both monetary and non-monetary such as power

- recognition, both intrinsic and achievement;

- confidence

- self-esteem

Self-esteem—how you feel about yourself—is the most crucial and important element of psychological maturity to influence. Remember the play and movie *My Fair Lady*? Eliza Doolittle went from a flower girl to a lady based on a bet between two gentlemen. One of the men felt that with the proper training, he could pass off a street pauper as a lady in societal circles. He did and won the bet!

There are four types of followers. They are classified as:

- R1, who is low on ability and low on motivation. This person doesn't have the job skills and doesn't want to do anything.

- R2, who is low on ability and high on motivation. This person wants to do the job, but might be new and in need of training.

- R3, who is high on ability and low on motivation. This person knows the job, but has lost his or her drive and doesn't want to do it anymore.

- R4, who is high on ability and high on motivation. This is the star performer who is already motivated and gets results.

4 TYPES OF FOLLOWERS

- R1 Low on Ability, Low on Motivation

- R2 Low on Ability, High on Motivation

- R3 High on Ability, Low on Motivation

- R4 High on Ability, High on Motivation

How do you as the leader communicate with the followers? Based on tasks and relations, the communication will be either one way or two way. Two-way communication is driven by the follower behavior; the leader drives one-way communication.

How to Communicate

Two-Way Communication	Two-Way Communication	One-Way Communication	One-Way Communication
Follower-Driven Behavior	*Follower-Driven Behavior*	*Leader-Driven Behavior*	*Leader-Driven Behavior*
Delegate	Support	Guide	Tell
R4 High Ability High Motivation	**R3** High Ability Low Motivation	**R2** Low Ability High Motivation	**R1** Low Ability Low Motivation

Type of Follower (R1-R4)

The lowest level of maturity—R1—equals the tell/direct or hands-on approach. The highest level of maturity—R4—equals delegate or hands-off approach.

For example, an R4 follower has high ability and high motivation. The leader would leave this person alone because any help would be perceived as negative. The leader would delegate and follow up at certain agreed-upon milestones. With an R3 follower—who has high ability and low motivation—the leader would be supportive saying, "You can do it; I know you can." With an R2 follower—someone with low ability and high motivation—the leader would guide or coach. The leader could build self-esteem in this follower by referring to a time when the person did a good job. The R1 follower—someone with low ability and low motivation—would need to be told or directed what to do. The leader would need to keep close tabs on the progress of the task.

There is an exception. Leaders under adverse conditions, such as a building on fire, imminent danger or crisis will probably resort to "telling" because the style used is driven by the needs of the follower. Also, a person can be in one area and move to another based on a reorganization, leadership change, or personal crisis.

Once you understand your management or leadership style and the style of your Followers, to effectively lead, you must determine the order of events to accomplish the goals.

ORDER OF EVENTS ...

1. **Determine Task / Function**

2. **Assess Level of Readiness**

3. **Match the Appropriate Leadership Style**

4. **Monitor Closely or From a Distance**

Matching the appropriate leadership style can be characterized as S1 tell/direct; S2 guide/coach; S3 supportive; and S4 delegate.

ASSESSMENT EVALUATION

		S1	S2	S3	S4
	R4				XXXX
READINESS (FOLLOWER)	R3	*OVER*	*LEADING*	XXXX	
	R2		XXXX		
	R1	XXXX	*UNDER*	*LEADING*	
		S1 Tell	**S2** Guide	**S3** Support	**S4** Delegate
			LEADERSHIP STYLE		

XXXX indicates where the employee is. For example, the employee in the lower left box XXXX that is above the S1 and right of the R1 has limited ability and limited will. As the leader, you would use the tell style and focus on the task. If you try to guide, support, or delegate, you are under leading, which will not result in the desired outcome.

The XXXX above the S2 and right of the R2 has limited ability and wants to do the task. You would guide and train this person. If you tell this person, you are over leading; if you support or delegate, you are under leading.

The XXXX above the S3 and right of the R3 has high ability and limited will to do the job. As the leader, be supportive and try to bring up the person's confidence level. This person may have been in the position for some time and needs to know that what he does is of value. If you tell or guide, you are over leading; if you delegate, you are under leading.

The XXXX above the S4 and right of the R4 has high ability and high will. Delegate and empower and leave this person alone. If you try to tell, guide, or support this person, you are over leading. It is better to under lead than over lead.

Motivation needs to be flexible to situational needs and driven by the follower needs.

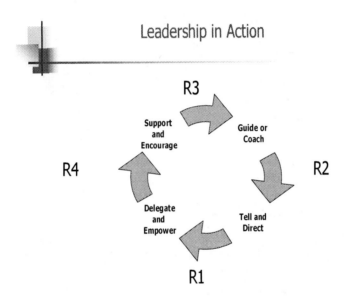

Telling or directing behaviors include:

- stating objectives and define tasks
- setting standards and timetables
- monitoring performance
- demanding compliance
- request timely responses
- being clear and specific

Guiding or coaching behaviors include:

- explaining procedure
- providing rationale for discussion mode
- reviewing for understanding
- setting parameters
- encouraging practicing
- exploring options and consequences
- asking questions; probing and agreeing on outcomes
- consulting, but with you as the leader making the decision

Supporting behaviors include:

- discussing your concerns and leveling with the person
- taking responsibility for your share of the problem
- letting the other person vent
- encouraging disclosure; saying "Tell me more"
- probing to uncover concerns
- praising previous performance
- exploring solutions jointly
- confirming roles and expectations
- following up at agreed-upon intervals

Delegating or empowering behaviors include:

- turn the followers loose
- responding to their requests
- staying out of the picture; not mingling
- being available
- being ready to change your approach

What happens if the person has a crisis, there is a reorganization, or leadership changes? Use the supportive behaviors in regressive situations. The key behaviors include:

- Disclose: Reveal your concerns and own your share of the problem.

- Listen: Empathize and let the follower "vent."

- Discuss: Encourage disclosure; probe to uncover their concerns.

- Support: Praise previous performance.

- Explore Solutions: Jointly participate; seek a "win-win" solution.

- Encourage action: Confirm roles and expectations.

I want to bring to your attention what de-motivates a work group—office romances. I have witnessed several office romances. One was between a high-level manager and a mid level-manager; one of them was married. They told one person—supposedly in confidence. That one person told another, and that person told another. Before long, people were whispering about the two of them. In the end, the high-level manager lost his job, his family suffered tremendously from the affair, and the mid-level manager lost respect and trust from all the people she knew. This type of behavior shows disrespect for others in the workplace. People believe that if you lie about this, you may be lying about other things. It creates resentful or jealous employee(s). You could even have some innocent coworkers get negatively involved if they are asked to cover up the whereabouts of the romantic individuals during office hours. The workplace may experience low morale, high sick leave use, low productivity, loss of loyalty, and diminished integrity resulting in loss of trust or even sexual harassment litigation against the company and individual.

In summary, motivation is best done in a safe and secure environment where you have respectful relationships. You cannot motivate an employee, but you can positively impact the environment that will lead to the employee's motivation. A leader is a follower is a leader. Remember, **effective leadership is situational and must be flexible to use all styles based on the needs of the follower**.

Chapter 12: How to Analyze Organizational Effectiveness **and** Manage an Organization

In Chapters 1 and 2, I referred to the McKenzie Model 7S and other tools used to analyze organizational efficiency and effectiveness. This chapter gives two examples of how to use these tools and discusses the benefit of doing an organizational intervention.

While employed by a large business, I had the opportunity to analyze ways to reduce the hourly rate charged back to the department for in-house services rendered. The skills and expertise within the department were highly regarded and critical to innovation and the company's success.

The goal was to implement streamlined and improved processes and procedures to eliminate redundancies and provide efficiencies without losing effectiveness. There were three alternatives. The first two included three scenarios: 100 percent funding with current resources; 75 percent funding and reduced resources; and 25 percent funding and reduced resources that would be assigned to critical projects only. Alternative One was to remain at the current off-site location with internal support and external resources for specialized technical skills. Alternative Two was to move the department to a central onsite location and provide internal support and external resources for specialized technical skills. Alternative Three was to do nothing. Here are the processes that I followed.

The first step was to identify the problem. Why was there a need for the organizational intervention? The indicators were that the internal cost per hour was not competitive with the same service that the unit could contract from external resources. In addition, new legislation changed and significantly reduced funding sources from external organizations, resulting in future higher cost per hour for internal services.

I met with the department leadership and defined the parameters or scope of the study. They wanted to understand what projects and what resources would be available at 100 percent funding, at 75 percent funding, and at 25 percent funding. In addition, they wanted to know the impact of remaining at the current location with the higher anticipated lease costs versus moving the department to a central location where the lease costs would be spread among several other departments. The project was to be completed within ninety days.

The next step was to develop the history of the department. I met with the leadership to find out what they wanted their department to accomplish. Their mission was to provide timely and relevant technology information to guide business decisions. This department was a key component for the company's ability to be one of the nation's leading suppliers of its product. In developing the department's history, it turned out that a new state law had changed the way this department had received funding, resulting in a significant reduction of funding. The department needed to investigate alternative funding sources. The product this department provided was critical to the company's future.

The next step was to identify the business strategy. The company wanted to continue to invest in new areas and technologies. This department provided timely and relevant technology information to guide the company's decisions by identifying, evaluating, and delivering technologies consistent with the business strategies. This department also played a key role in the company's ability to maintain market share and provide high quality, timely and valued services.

The next step was to develop an operating plan for the department that included the mission, vision, goals, and objectives. The leadership decided that excellent service, operating efficiency and asset utilization were the key strategies required to achieve the vision and mission of the department. I asked how the department would achieve excellent service. The leaders decided that they needed to improve the value and competitiveness of their products and services. To achieve operating efficiency, they decided that they needed to use innovative work practices and rigorous cost control. And, for asset utilization, they wanted to improve the productivity and use of their assets.

The next step was to determine how the goals would be met. I developed three objectives: improve the value of the department and competitiveness of the products and services; improve operating efficiency; and improve asset utilization. To achieve the first objective, a client satisfaction survey was developed to find out what was working; what wasn't working; and if the client could change one thing, what would it be and why. To improve operating efficiency, I used the McKinsey Model 7S to develop an analysis of strengths, weaknesses, opportunities, and threats, commonly called a SWOT analysis. To improve asset utilization, the technology group developed a database to manage assets.

Mission: Provide timely and relevant technology information to guide business decisions.		
Vision: Continue to invest into new areas and technologies to provide timely and relevant technology information to guide the company's decisions by identifying, evaluating, and delivering technologies consistent with the business strategies.		

Strategy	**Goals**	**Objectives**
Excellent Service	Improve value and competitiveness of products and services.	Use results from client satisfaction surveys to identify needed improvements.
Operating Efficiency	Improve operating efficiency by using innovative work practices and rigorous cost control.	Analyze staffing, skills, structure, systems, style, strategies, and shared values.
Asset Utilization	Improve utilization of assets.	Improve usage of information technology to manage assets.

I developed the client satisfaction survey that follows.

Client Satisfaction Survey Question Comments	
What is working?	
What is not working?	
Why is it not working?	
If you could change one thing, what would it be?	
Why would you change it?	
How would you change it?	

From this survey, I developed two lists.

The first list encompassed what wasn't working. The second list comprised the changes that the employees wanted, including why they would make the changes and sometimes how they thought the changes might work better. The second list was further broken into what could be done right now, what could be done in the near future with minimal expense, and what could be done in the long term that might be more costly. What could be done now and in the near future with minimal expense was considered in the evaluation of the organization.

The next step was to analyze the internal environment's strengths and weaknesses. The strengths included: knowledgeable and expert employees; accurate financial information; proactive technological support for the computer intensive environment; and, database to track projects. The weaknesses included: high operating costs; slow turnaround time and insufficient staffing for contracts; poorly defined roles for some employees; inaccurate and cumbersome database information for contracts; and inability to track royalties and patent rights.

The next step was to analyze the external environment—opportunities and threats. Opportunities included: size staff to meet client needs; reduce operating costs by eliminating duplicate and unnecessary work; define and streamline processes to gain efficiencies; install technology to improve availability; support writing or documenting reports; and facilitate or consult to increase productivity. Threats included: increased competition; changing client needs and expectations; funding resources; contracting done in other departments of the company; and the ability to hire and retain future skills required.

Next, I developed the SWOT analysis—strengths, weaknesses, opportunities, and threats. The department had an excellent opportunity for future growth and profitability. It was critical to the company's success.

The department had excellent expertise and highly qualified employees. The technology group was proactive and provided excellent and timely service. The contract group had new supervision and support personnel who reviewed the contracting practices and processes to streamline and reduce turnaround time.

The department was positioning itself to lower operating costs because of competition. By defining and streamlining processes and eliminating redundant activities and products that did not add value, this unit expected to lower operating costs and improve efficiencies.

While some believed that centralizing contracting made sense for routine and standard types of contracts, the overall consensus was that this unit's contracts dealt with intellectual assets that should probably remain in this unit. It was suggested that this department work with the legal department to develop standard service contracts for intellectual assets.

Lastly, there was an imbalance of human resources supply and demand for the highly skilled computer and technology contracting. Even though the company encouraged the staffers to upgrade their skills, few employees actually continued to do so. As a result, many employees wanted to do well, but they lacked the technical skills required in a competitive environment. **Employees must be encouraged to continue education and advance their current skills**.

After the SWOT analysis, I completed a business assessment, analyzing the strategy, structure, systems, style, staffing, skills, and shared values.

Strategy is how a unit rates against its competitive environment to achieve a sustainable competitive advantage. This unit had high costs for the service provided. The employees were knowledgeable in their work. The clients were surveyed to measure client satisfaction and needs. The unit was benchmarked against outside competition to better utilize resources.

Structure is the specialization and integration that is influenced primarily by the strategy and organization size and diversity. Contracts were unique due to royalties and intellectual property rights, including patents, copyrights, and trade secrets. The unit had accounting expertise for financial analysis. The technology area was proactive and supported a computer intensive environment. The department valued the unit's services and products. The unit appeared to be risk adverse.

In analyzing the structure, I found that the nature of the work required the need for internal capabilities and control to assure prompt responses and quality services.

The systems facet represents the procedures, information systems, performance measures, rewards, budgets, and controls that support the strategy and structure. Contract monitoring was ineffective because the process took too long. The forms were long and cumbersome. Financial information was too detailed, including too many reports. Computer and information technology was proactive and met client needs. The unit provided excellent search capabilities. The database was useful but cumbersome, resulting in most people not using it. Better guidelines for writing contracts were needed.

In analyzing systems, I found that the contracting process needed to be streamlined and standardized for routine types of contracts, including having a database that was meaningful and useful. I recommended that only mandatory financial reports be retained. The technology section had the expertise for the work required. It was recommended only using highly skilled external resources when needing to augment current resources.

Style describes what is done, not what is said by leadership. Style is how managers spend their time. What I found was that the squeaky wheel got the contracting work first. The autocratic leadership style needed to move toward a facilitative, leadership role.

Staffing determines if you have the right resources for the work needs. I matched the resources for each of the three scenarios for each alternative, reducing redundant and obsolete personnel.

The skills area identifies a company's basic competencies. The technology, contract, and financial and budgeting personnel all had the required competencies and skill levels

In analyzing staffing and skills, I found that the department had a continuous training program and paid tuition to encourage employees to continue upgrading their education and skills. Most took advantage of these benefits.

The concept of shared values describes the level of trust, integrity, morale, motivation, and culture of an organization. Morale was low due to the uncertainty of the department and unit's future. Future funding source issues caused anxiety and low trust. I found from interviews with key employees and from client satisfaction surveys that the unit's work was valued and an integral and necessary part of the department's success. The skills and expertise of the unit's personnel were highly regarded.

After management reviewed the summary of my findings, they chose Alternative Two to gain economies without losing efficiencies. The critical projects and personnel were moved to a centralized location. The rental lease for the previous location was cancelled. Only resources who were working on the critical projects were retained; others were either placed in other departments in the company or given severance packages. Overall, the company realized a $1.1 million savings and a significant reduction of the cost per hour for work produced which was a competitive advantage for future product and services.

Later, I worked for a small business that had had five employees. Two resigned abruptly and another left within two weeks. The pressing issue was that the processes had not been documented and there was no one to do the work. We had one week to train, document and flow-chart processes and procedures, and determine the resources required to stay in business.

With minimal knowledge of the business and a strong determination to see if what I learned about managing organizations worked for small as well as large companies, I embraced the opportunity. First, I met with the owner to discuss the core business. We determined the product and why the supply was important. We identified the customers who wanted the product and created demand. We identified the resources. We also talked about his vision for the future of the business.

The mission of the company was a pure equity lender who matched borrower needs with lender needs. The company's vision was to provide the best competitive services and products while attaining a profit and maintaining shareholder value. After developing the mission and vision, we developed the strategies—excellent service, operating efficiency and asset utilization.

Next up were the goals. For excellent service, the goal was to improve staffing by hiring the right resources to match borrower needs and lender needs; for operating efficiency, to use innovative work practices and **document** those practices; for asset utilization, to improve use of assets.

We then discussed the objectives. I used the McKinsey Model 7S for organizational effectiveness by analyzing the company's staffing, skills, structure, systems, style, strategies, and shared values.

Finally, we completed a SWOT analysis to determine the strengths, weaknesses, opportunities, and threats.

Mission: A pure equity lender who matches borrower needs with lender needs.

Vision: Provide the best competitive services and products while attaining a profit and maintaining shareholder value.

Strategy	Goals	Objectives
Excellent Service	Improve staffing by hiring the right resources to match borrower needs and lender needs.	Determine required skills; identify and hire needed resources.
Operating Efficiency	Improve operating efficiency by using innovative work practices and documenting those practices.	Analyze staffing, skills, structure, systems, style, strategies, and shared values.
Asset Utilization	Improve utilization of assets.	Improve usage of information technology to manage assets.

From the analysis and research, the owner and I brainstormed and developed an action plan for the three days that I had to receive training from the two previous employees. An action plan is a step-by-step process, outlining what needs to be done, by whom and by when to accomplish the desired result. It is similar to a roadmap that lists all the streets and intersections that gets you from point A to point B.

Category	Action Steps	Time Needed	Who	Date	Notes
Computer Systems	Define all systems and use of each.	3 hrs	Sam	8/1	
Forms & Labels	Identify all forms, labels, and letters. Sample of each.	2 hrs	Sam	8/1	
Office Administration	Define opening, operating, closing office. Document processes.	3 hrs	Sam	8/1	
Daily Activities— Loan Processing	Define daily activities. Flow-chart processes; develop samples.	4 hrs	Joan	8/2	
Daily Activities— Loan Servicing	Define daily activities. Flow-chart processes; develop samples.	4 hrs	Mary	8/2	
Daily Activities— Partnerships	Define daily activities. Flow-chart processes; develop samples.	4 hrs	Joan	8/3	
Quarterly & Annual Activities	Define and document all activities.	5 hrs	Bob	8/4	

The immediate need was to write down and flow-chart all processes for day-to-day work activities. From the key activities identified, we developed action plans for immediate and future needs.

At the same time, we identified all the key activities and resources that were pertinent to the business. The results of the analysis included: systems, implement a financial software system for partnerships and upgrade technology; staffing, hire a licensed employee to sell the product; and skills, obtain the necessary licenses to manage the business and write a procedures manual documenting the office procedures and processes.

A year later, all the processes and procedures were flow-charted and documented, which facilitated and provided consistency in training employees. We have now retired and sold the business to private individuals at the appraised value before the employees' departure. All the processes and procedures were well documented, which facilitated the ease in which the new owners and personnel were trained. It's rewarding to be able to walk away from a thirty-six-year-old business and know that it will continue to run successfully.

With the use of an organizational effectiveness tool for analysis as well as the use of action plans to identify tasks step-by-step, you can analyze, recommend changes, and monitor progress of changes for the successful operation of any organization, big or small, profit or nonprofit.

References

Bennis, Warren. (1989). <u>On Becoming A Leader</u>. Menlo Park, California: Addison-Wesley Publishing Company.

Bick, Julie. (1997). "All I Really Need to Know in Business I Learned at Microsoft." <u>Inside Strategies to Help You Succeed</u>. New York, NP: Pocket Books, A Division of Simon & Shuster, Inc.

Birch, David L., Haggerty, A., and Parsons, W. (1997). "Corporate Demographics. Entrepreneurial Hot Spots." <u>The Best Places in America to Start and Grow A Company</u>. Conneticut: Cognetics, Inc.

Block, P. (1993). <u>Stewardship</u>. San Francisco, CA: Berrett-Kochler Publishers.

Bridges, William, Ph.D. (1992). "Transitions." <u>Making Sense of Life's Changes</u>." Menlo Park, California: Addison-Wesley Publishing Company.

Bridges, William, Ph.D. (1992). <u>Surviving Corporate Transition</u>. Mill Valley, California: William Bridges & Associates.

Bull, James R. (1997). <u>DNA Leadership Through Goal-Driven Management</u>. Reston, Virginia: The Goals Institution.

Burke, W. Warner. (1987). <u>Organizational Development</u>. Menlo Park, California: Addison-Wesley Publishing Company.

Champy, James. (1995). "Reengineering Management." <u>The Mandate for New Leadership: Managing the</u>

Change to the Reengineered Corporation. New York, NY: Harper Business

Collins, James C. & Porras, Jerry I. (1997). "Built to Last." Successful Habits of Visionary Companies. New York, NY: Harper Collins Publisher, Inc.

Coombs, Jeff & Tulgan, Bruce. (July 1977). Generation X: *The Workforce of the Future.* Nineteenth Edition. Copyright 1997, Rainmaker, Inc.

Covey, Stephen R. (1994). First Things First. New York, NY: Simon & Schuster, pp. 103-117.

Covey, Stephen R. (1989). "The 7 Habits of Highly Effective People." Powerful Lessons in Personal Change. New York, NY: Simon & Schuster Publisher.

DePree, M. (1989). Leadership Without Power. San Francisco, CA: Jossey-Bass Publishers.

Drucker, Peter F. (1985). The Effective Executive. New York, NY: Harper & Row Publishers, Inc.

Gerber, Michael E. (1995). The E Myth. New York, NY: Harper Collins Publisher, Inc.

Goleman, Daniel. (1995). Emotional Intelligence. New York, NY: Bantam Books.

Greiner, Larry E. & Schein, Virginia E. (1989). Power and Organizational Development. Menlo Park, California: Addison-Wesley Publishing Company.

Grove, Andrew. (1996). Only the Paranoid Survive. New York, NY: Doubleday & Company.

Hill, Charles W. L. & Jones, Garth R. (1989). <u>Strategic Management Theory</u>. New York, NY: Houghton Mifflin Co.

Jager, Rama D. & Ortiz, Rafael (1997). "In the Company of Giants." <u>Candid Conversations with the Visionary Companies of the Digital World</u>. New York, NY: McGraw-Hill.

Kotter, John P. (1990). <u>A Force for Change</u>. New York, NY: The Free Press.

Kotter, John P. & Heskett, J. L. (1992). <u>Corporate Culture and Performance</u>. New York, NY: The Free Press.

Kouzes, James M. & Posner, Barry Z. (1997). <u>The Leadership Challenge</u>. San Francisco, California: Jossey-Bass Publishers.

Leider, Richard & Shapiro, David A. (1995). <u>Repacking Your Bags: Lighten Your Load for the Rest of Your Life</u>. New York, NY: Hyperion.

Micklethwait, John & Woolridge, Adrian. (1996). "The Witch Doctors." <u>Making Sense of Management Gurus</u>. New York, NY: Random House, Inc.

Nelson, Bob. (1997). <u>1001 Ways to Energize Employees</u>. New York, NY: Workman Publishing.

Nichols, M. P. & Schwartz, R. C. (1995). <u>Family Therapy</u>: Conceps and Methods (3rd Edition). Netham Heights: Allyn and Bacon.

O'Neil, John R. (1994). "The Paradox of Success." <u>When Winning at Work Means Losing at Life</u>. New York, NY: G. P. Putnam's Sons.

Peters, T. and Waterman, R. H., Jr. (1982). In Search of Excellence. New York, NY: Warner Books, Inc.

Pritchett, Price. (1996). "Mindshift." Understanding the Changing World of Work. Dallas, TX: Pritchett & Associates.

Schein, Edgar. (1992). Organizational Culture and Leadership. (2nd Edition). San Francisco, CA: Jossey-Bass Publishers.

Senge, Peter M. (1990). "The Fifth Discipline." The Art and Practice of the Learning Organization. New York, NY: Currency and Doubleday.

Senge, Peter M. (1994). The Fifth Discipline Fieldbook. New York, NY: Doubleday.

Silver, A. David. (1995). "Quantum Companies." 100 Companies That Will Change the Face of Tomorrow's Business. Princeton, NJ: Peterson's/Pacesetter Books.

Southern, N. (Winter 1997). Transformative Learning Across Cultures: Creating opportunities for learning and relationships through communicative competence. Vision/Action. San Francisco, CA, pp 17-20.

Yalom, Irvin D. (1995). "The Theory and Practice of Group Psychology." New York, NY: Basic Books, A Division of Harper Collins Publishers, Inc., pp. 20-21, 295-303.

Other

McKinsey & Company is an international management
consulting firm that advised top management of
leading organizations on issues of strategy,
organization and operations. The 7-S Model is used
to help clients make substantial and lasting
improvements in their performance and build a firm
that is able to attract, develop, excite, motivate, and
retain exceptional people. (www.mckinsey.com)

Myers Briggs Type Personality Preference instrument is one
of the most widely used tools in businesses around
the world and has been in existence for more than 60
years.

A special thanks to the fast growing companies in Northern
California during the 1990's: Applied Materials,
Incorporated; Atmel Corporation; Chiron
Corporation; Cisco Sytems, Incorporated; Foundation
Health Corporation; Hewlett-Packard; Infinity
Financial;, Microsoft Corporation; The Money Store;
S3, Incorporated; Silicon Graphics; and, Solectron
Corporation.

On-Line Search Including Internet/World Wide Web.